CW00763419

FIRESTRIKE

Falcon SAS Thrillers
Book Two

Robert Charles

SAPERE
BOOKS

FIRESTRIKE

Published by Sapere Books.

20 Windermere Drive, Leeds, England, LS17 7UZ,
United Kingdom

saperebooks.com

ISBN: 978-1-80055-481-8

CHAPTER 1

'What I am afraid of,' Harry Killian said quietly, 'is what could prove to be the biggest and most spectacular terrorist operation ever launched. Compared to this every other terrorist atrocity the world has ever seen could all fade into insignificance.'

The words hung heavy and sombre in the comfortable study of Killian's Surrey home. It signalled the end of the casual after-dinner conversation that had lingered until Mary Killian had made her polite excuses and retired to bed. She had obviously known that her husband had something important on his mind.

Killian had only one listener. Both of them were seated in large leather armchairs, facing each other over cigars and brandy, and at first sight they were a complete contrast.

Colonel Harry Killian was in his sixties, he wore a black eyepatch and his left shirtsleeve was carefully folded up and pinned back behind the stump of his missing left arm. His one remaining blue eye gleamed sharp and clear, revealing the still dynamic mind behind the damaged body.

His companion and dinner guest was twenty years his junior; a tall, lean young man who had reached that golden age when emotional maturity and a wide range of human experience formed the perfect balance for a body at the peak of physical fitness. He had been relaxed, but now his interest sharpened.

Mark Falcon had known Harry Killian for many years. They had both been members of the elite Special Air Service Regiment. Killian had begun his career during World War Two, becoming one of the founder members of the S.A.S., and serving in virtually all its campaigns until he had been blown up in a Land Rover during the desert war in Oman in the early nineteen seventies. It was there that he had lost his arm and an eye.

The then Captain Mark Falcon had been his escort on that mission. Despite being badly injured himself Falcon had held off a group of fanatical hostile tribesmen until a search and rescue party had arrived many hours later. It had been the beginning of a long friendship.

Killian had never returned to active service with the S.A.S., but his knowledge and experience were still of infinite value and eventually he had been found a desk job with British Intelligence. For Falcon the war in Oman had also come to an end. While he languished in hospital recovering from his injuries the entire team he had led through three campaigns had been wiped out when their helicopter had been shot down over the arid mountains. Falcon had gone on to serve two more duty tours in Northern Ireland, but he had never led another squad. The old team had been irreplaceable. He had preferred to volunteer for undercover missions alone, and when he had proved himself again to his own satisfaction, he too had resigned his commission.

Now he was a freelance journalist and author, but from time to time he did favours for Harry Killian.

Their relationship was one of mutual trust, beliefs and ideals. Most of all they shared the same philosophy: a conviction that those who had been gifted with greater strength and abilities had a duty toward their fellow men, a direct responsibility to help defend the rest of mankind from the brute forces of human evil.

Mark Falcon possessed the whole wealth of S.A.S. skills. He had been trained in every anti-terrorist technique and in every aspect of jungle, desert and urban warfare. He had also been blessed with high intelligence and a creative and enquiring mind that had made him extremely successful in his new career. His first book, a detailed study of terrorism and guerrilla warfare throughout the world, had become a rare bestseller. Practically every copy had been bought up by the various military and intelligence departments throughout the Western world. Since then Falcon had made a name for himself as a photo-journalist on remote and crisis-spot assignments for an international news and travel magazine.

It was this ability to go anywhere, and often to be in the hottest trouble spot at a crucial time, which made him invaluable to Harry Killian. Falcon was his own master now, Killian could give him no orders, but if Killian asked for help then Falcon would never hesitate to respond.

Now Killian was obviously worried, and if Harry Killian had cause for deep concern, then the world had cause to tremble.

Falcon said calmly. 'Harry, I think you'd best tell me about it.'

Killian leaned forward in his chair. 'Let me fill in the background. You probably know it all as well as I do, but it will do no harm to refresh your memory. A few years ago a West German business consortium which called itself OTRAG established an independent rocket launching facility in Africa. Their aim was to send up observation and communications satellites — spy satellites — for any Third World country which could pay their price.'

'In 1978 OTRAG were operating from an isolated plateau in Zaire.' Falcon helped him along. 'I went out there and wrote a feature article for the *Empire News Service*. It was a fantastic set-up. They had leased an area the size of Colorado from the

Zaire government. The launch site was inaccessible except by air, and they were ruling the whole area as though it was their own private colony. Since then they've had to leave Zaire, and they've now set up again in Libya.'

'Exactly,' Killian nodded his head. 'The huge size of the area OTRAG controlled, and the way they were running it, was so much like old-style colonialism that they had to get out. The left-wing African states raised a howl of protest. Moscow accused them of running a secret NATO base, and the West German government finally got cold feet and persuaded the Zaire government to kick them out. OTRAG spent a couple of years looking for a new site, but now they're in business again in the Libyan desert fifty miles south of Tripoli.'

'And that's what worries you,' Falcon guessed. 'The fact that Colonel Gaddafi might have his finger on the firing button?'

'Mark, nobody can be happy with the OTRAG operation in Libya. But it's not my biggest worry. Now there's something more ominous, a dangerous new step in the proliferation of private rocket sites.'

'Then you must be talking about Project *Vulcan*.'

Killian nodded again and puffed briefly on his cigar. 'I knew it wouldn't have escaped your notice. *Vulcan* has been set up by an East German aeronautics company, supposedly in competition with OTRAG. They've established their site in a remote area of cleared jungle in Mozambique. Again the claim is that the enterprise is entirely peaceful in purpose. The East Germans are pointing to the EUROPE space centre in Guiana in South America, and the OTRAG operation in Libya, and saying that their entry into the race is simply to prevent Western business interests from gaining an unfair monopoly in private space shots.'

Falcon sipped his whisky thoughtfully. 'The East Germans couldn't have set up *Vulcan* without approval from Moscow. Which is a bit of bare-arsed cheek when you recall all the outrage they were pretending over the OTRAG operation in Zaire. *A nuclear knife aimed at the heart of Africa*! I seem to remember that as a cry from radio Moscow at the time.'

Killian smiled thinly. 'The Russians quietly dropped all their protests about OTRAG as soon as the West Germans moved to Libya. About *Vulcan* they've had nothing to say at all. Obviously rocket sites in innocent Africa are okay just so long as Moscow holds enough of the control strings.'

'So what about *Vulcan*? On the face of it it's a straight East German commercial project. We know Moscow must have prompted it behind the scenes, but if the Russians wanted they could quietly install military rockets in Mozambique without making themselves so obvious. As I see it *Vulcan* doesn't have to have any sinister purpose. It could be they are only interested in the hard currency that's waiting to change hands in what looks like being a very lucrative private satellite market.'

Killian sighed. 'I wish I could believe it was all so innocent, but there are other factors, Mark, which you don't know about.'

Falcon knew there had to be, because Killian still looked worried. They were going deeper now than Falcon's newsman's knowledge, and so he waited in silence for the older man to continue.

Killian's voice rasped again, taking on the hard edge which showed his concern. 'When OTRAG were operating in Zaire the CIA picked up some rumours. Nothing too substantial, but enough to raise the fear that the OTRAG launch site could become the target of a massive terrorist attack. Some of the rumours surfaced in Africa. They might have been dismissed as pure, wide-eyed ambition by some of the more naive guerrilla groups down there, but we got some hints coming out of Eastern Europe too. The KGB pulls most of the terrorist strings around the world, so we had to start taking the whole thing seriously.

'In the end it came to nothing. If the official protest campaign aimed at OTRAG was a blind then the Russians overdid it. OTRAG got their marching orders out of Zaire, and the terrorist attack, if there was one planned, was forestalled before it started.'

'But you think there was an attack planned?'

'Right.'

'But for obvious reasons it won't be switched to OTRAG's new base in Libya.'

'Right again. OTRAG setting up in Libya must have been a bonus for the Russians. It's created a huge headache and plenty of sleepless nights for Western security chiefs, while the Russians know they can closely monitor the whole operation through their Libyan allies. The big disadvantage for the KGB is that they can't allow a terrorist operation to be directed into Libya. For one thing they won't want to damage the image of an ally as important as Gaddafi. And for another it would probably have been the Libyans who would have directed the attack in Zaire, so with OTRAG now in their ruler's pocket they would have no need.'

Falcon was beginning to understand. He said softly, 'So you suspect that the East Germans have only been allowed to set up *Vulcan* to provide an alternative target.'

'That's it.' Killian's face was grim. 'Something was planned. Something the KGB still wants to see happen. It can't happen to OTRAG, because by an ironic twist they've moved themselves to what is probably the only safe location in Africa. So behind the scenes Moscow has set up *Vulcan*.'

'Then *Vulcan* is a blind.'

'No, Mark, *Vulcan* is genuine, I'm sure of that. The East German businessmen who have put up the money and expertise are doing exactly what they claim to be doing — making a determined attempt to capture part of the future commercial satellite market. They must have been both surprised and delighted when Moscow didn't block their project, but I can't imagine that they have any knowledge of why they were given the freedom to go ahead. In the same way I'm sure the Mozambique government has had no prior warning of why they have been encouraged to play host country to the East Germans. Both parties will appear to be victims, and they will be victims, of whatever is planned.'

'And what do you think is planned?'

'The beer talk originally picked up in Zaire was that a guerrilla army was going to capture the facility. If that should happen now to *Vulcan*, then at the least it will be a massive propaganda spectacular for black Marxist terrorists. At the worst—'

He left it unfinished, helplessly shrugging his shoulders.

'I see what you mean,' Falcon said softly. 'A rocket is just a rocket — a glorified transport vehicle. It becomes commercial or military depending upon how you load it and where you aim it.'

Killian looked straight at his young friend. '*Vulcan* are firing their first test rocket in two weeks' time,' he said casually. 'And I understand that a select group of the world's press corps has been invited to attend.'

Falcon smiled broadly. He took out his wallet and removed a square of printed card which he offered for inspection.

'The *Empire News Service* has been invited to send one journalist,' he affirmed. '*Vulcan* are laying on a private jet from Salisbury to fly twenty of us into the launch site.'

Killian returned the card with an even wider smile. 'Mark, I was hoping you could somehow get a ticket to that launch party. I might have guessed you would already have one in your pocket.'

'I take it you want me to make a discreet check on security down there? Figure out how the place could be taken, and what could be done to prevent it?'

'That was the general idea. You're the ideal man for the job, with genuine press qualifications.'

'Of course I'll do it.' There was no hesitation, but then he paused for a moment before increasing the offer. 'I have no other commitments between now and the date of the launch, so I could go into Africa now. That'll give me a couple of weeks to do some digging, maybe in Salisbury, Lusaka, or Maputo.'

'Johannesburg,' Killian advised firmly.

He leaned forward in his chair. 'I've seen all the CIA reports on the likely possibilities. There's only one terrorist force in that part of the world which is big enough and sufficiently well organized to do the job. They call themselves *Black K*. Their leader is a man named Jonas Kitaka.'

'I've heard of him, a Marxist intellectual, pretty ruthless even by terrorist standards.'

'He's ruthless all right. He started his military career as a soldier in the South African Army, but got out when he found it was entirely white-officered with no future for a black man. He next appeared fighting for one of the mercenary commandos in the Congo. He made sergeant, but it seems he killed other black men simply to learn more about white military skills and tactics. More recently he's attended Moscow-backed terrorist training camps in Mozambique, so he's had all the advantages of the best possible schooling from both sides.'

Falcon was searching through the files of his memory. 'Isn't he also something of a personality cult?'

'Right again. It's reflected in the name of his organization, and it's alienated him from most of the other guerrilla leaders. They think that most of his Marxism got rubbed off somewhere along the way, and that now he's just plain power-hungry. But he's got a lot of support, and he's the biggest thorn there is in the side of South African security. They believe he masterminded the terrorist bomb attacks on the Secunda and Sasolburg oil refineries.'

'And you think Kitaka is now in Johannesburg?'

'Nobody knows where he is. But it's as good a place as any to start. During the Congo war Kitaka was teamed with another sergeant, a white South African mercenary named Mike Kyller. I can give you Kyller's present address in Johannesburg. He might be able to give you some ideas.'

'Mike Kyller,' Falcon mused thoughtfully. 'I interviewed a mercenary named Kyller some years ago in Angola. It could be the same man.'

Harry Killian smiled warmly. 'Mark-my-boy, I knew all along that this job was tailor-made just for you.'

CHAPTER 2

The vast North African sandscape of the Libyan desert scorched under the fierce blaze of the high, white sun. A dry wind blew the hot, stinging dust over the wasteland of dunes and burning red rocks.

The OTRAG rocket standing erect on its launch pad dominated the nearby control centre, the radar screens, and the scattered assembly, accommodation and administration buildings. A gleaming white, elegant, sharp-finned pencil of tapering steel, it was based on a design principle derived from the V2 developed by Von Braun at Peenemunde.

Basically it was a cheap rocket, constructed from mass-produced commercial components. Its basic units were two fuel tanks and a series of twin-engine modules clustered in stages. The separate components had been purchased from a wide range of sources on the European market, and only assembled in their final form here in Libya. It was a neat way to bypass the West German and other European laws and regulations which were designed to restrict the export of military and potentially military hardware.

A large number of Libyan government officials and military officers had assembled to watch the launch, all of them listening attentively to the West German directors and technicians who were patiently explaining what was happening.

Two men who were part of this group stood carefully distant from the rest. One was a handsome young Arab in the uniform of a Major in the Libyan Air Force. The other was an older man, a squat figure in a crumpled grey suit. His face was square with heavy jowls.

It was only during the past few months that Salem Sharif had returned to wearing his Air Force uniform, for he had spent the last five years with Libyan Intelligence. He had been one of Gaddafi's most trusted envoys to the terrorist organizations enjoying Libyan support throughout the world.

His companion was Colonel Arkadi Lissenko, the senior KGB officer from the Russian embassy in Tripoli. Lissenko was sweating and uncomfortable, and looked worried.

The countdown reached zero. The rocket engines ignited and a blaze of fire pushed the pointed column of steel up from the launch pad. It ascended slowly at first, then gathered speed as the roar of sound faded. Within a minute only the red fire of the exhaust remained visible, and then that too disappeared into the limitless blue.

The spy satellite would eventually orbit at 22,300 miles above the earth. At that height it would keep pace with the earth's rotation and in effect be fixed permanently above the line of the Libya and Egyptian frontier.

A thunder of cheers and hand-clapping applause greeted the announcement that the satellite was on target. Lissenko and Sharif removed their padded ear protectors with the rest, and under cover of the deafening noise of triumph the Russian moved his lips in a soft murmur.

'Well, my young friend, are you certain you know enough about this whole operation to advise effectively on project *Firestrike?*'

Sharif kept his face expressionless, hiding the distaste and distrust he was beginning to feel for this gross infidel who so obviously believed that all Arabs were both ignorant and expendable.

'I am a trained pilot,' he reminded Lissenko. 'I understand guidance systems and flight principles. Now I have studied every aspect of this operation, especially the launch countdown procedure and the means of installing the chosen payload. I could not build you such a rocket, but I would know if any of the technicians involved in the launching were to deviate from their proper task.'

'That should be sufficient,' Lissenko agreed.

He mopped more sweat from his glistening face, and for a moment his small eyes stared brightly over the handheld mask of his handkerchief.

'There is only one other important thing to remember. There will be no Russian or Cuban links with the final scenario we envisage in Mozambique. We have made sure that none of our own personnel or our Cuban allies are involved. And the only possible Libyan link will be yourself.'

'Do not concern yourself. I shall maintain a low profile.'

'Your profile must be invisible. You must restrict yourself to supervising the technical details where your newly acquired knowledge is essential. You must not involve yourself in any other area of the operation. Your face must be seen only by the smallest possible number of allies whom we can completely trust.'

'I am not a fool,' Sharif told him curtly. 'I know what I must, and what I must not, do.'

Lissenko realized that he had been tactless, and that he could not afford to offend this haughty young Arab.

'You will do well,' he soothed. 'Your record shows that your courage and intelligence have been proved many times. Colonel Gaddafi has personally recommended you for this mission.'

He paused, embarrassed by his own effluence, and then got back to reality. 'Are all your travel arrangements made?'

Sharif nodded, his contempt still carefully masked. 'I return to Tripoli with the rest of the observers. Tonight I shall be on an international flight to Karachi. From there I shall use my new Pakistani passport to fly to Zurich. From Zurich I fly to Zimbabwe. Contact will be made at my hotel, and from there I will be guided by the people of *Black K*.'

'Good, good.' Lissenko grunted approval even though he was still sweating and biting his lip. The roundabout route and the passport switch should effectively cover the Libyan's tracks, but still Lissenko could not help worrying. It gnawed into his soul like a dog's teeth on a bone.

He had schooled Sharif, so if the Arab made a mistake, then Lissenko knew that he would be blamed. The Arab would probably be dead, which was not so important. But his own fat neck would also be on the chopping block, and that was not a good feeling at all.

Falcon had returned to his London flat to catch a good night's sleep, and then made his final travel arrangements before taking a taxi to Heathrow. There, after two hours of waiting, he boarded a South African Airlines flight for Johannesburg. He passed Sharif high over North Africa. The Libyan was flying northward, while Falcon was southbound over neighbouring Algeria.

It was late in the evening when Falcon arrived at Jan Smuts International Airport. He called a taxi to take him into the sprawling, modern city of Johannesburg, at first sight an American-style skyscraper Metropolis which made it difficult to believe that he had been transported into Africa. The brief glimpses of neon night life might have been New York or Chicago, except that there were no black people on the crowded pavements. The black Africans had all been returned to their sullen townships outside the white-dominated city.

Falcon was too tired to even think about the irony of it all, and went straight to the huge *Transvaal Hotel* where he had reserved a room. His roving commission with ENS had made him an experienced air traveller, well acquainted with the problems of jet lag, and he had deliberately timed his arrival for the end of the day. It meant he could go straight to bed, and awaken after a full eight hours of normal sleep, refreshed and with his body clock carefully adjusted to face the new morning.

He showered and took his time over a leisurely breakfast. Afterward he went out shopping to supplement his sparse travelling wardrobe with some lightweight slacks and a few sports shirts. At the same time he picked up city maps and guides and a selection of local newspapers.

The headline story of the day was a series of sabotage explosions at several of South Africa's electrical power stations. They had been caused by Russian-made limpet mines and the human blame was generally attributed to the banned African National Congress. The reporting was matter-of-fact and unperturbed, the editorials seemed not to have noticed, and there was no mention of *Black K*.

Falcon spent most of the mid-day hours in a variety of bars, drinking sparingly and listening to the hub-bub of conversations floating around him. Few people seemed concerned by the latest wave of black terrorism, and those who mentioned it seemed to accept the sporadic demonstrations of black frustration as routine. The white community seemed complacent, fairly sure of itself, although a few people were arguing for more relaxation of petty apartheid.

Falcon returned to his hotel for a late lunch, and to study his maps and the layout of the city. The address Killian had given him for Mike Kyller was an apartment number in one of the towering blocks of the Hillbrow area. He checked with the telephone directory and had the satisfaction of seeing that Kyller was still there.

For a minute he considered the idea of simply dialling Kyller's number, but then decided that a face-to-face first contact would be best. Kyller might remember his face, but would probably not remember his name.

They had met briefly in Angola in 1976. Falcon had walked for two days through bush and jungle to find the small group of white mercenaries fighting for the southern-based UNITA army locked in the three-way struggle of civil war. He had talked for less than half an hour, mostly with the captain in command, and only for a few minutes with Kyller, before the interview had been abruptly terminated by a Cuban air attack.

After ducking the cannon shells from the buzzing MiG fighter Falcon found that the UNITA forces and their mercenary allies had wisely scattered, all of them melting invisibly into the thick bush. Only his panic-stricken guides remained, and they had immediately dragged him away to begin the forced march back the way they had come.

It was not much of a past association, but Falcon hoped it would be enough for Kyller to accept a drink and start talking over old times.

He took a taxi out to Hillbrow. He had not yet decided how long he might need to stay in Johannesburg, so he was not being too hasty in hiring a car.

On arrival he rode the elevator to the eighth floor of the ten-storey block. The doors opened on to wide corridors leading left, right, and straight ahead. The apartment he wanted, number 87, was down the corridor to his left. He knocked on the door and waited.

He had delayed his call until early evening, figuring this would be the best time to find Kyller at home, but after a minute it seemed that he was out of luck. He knocked again, more loudly, but there was no sound from inside.

Tentatively he tried the door. As he expected it was locked. He frowned as he contemplated using the plastic card in his wallet to ease open the simple Yale lock, but so far this was just a social call, and he decided it would be impolite to resort to burglary.

He turned away, resigned to the necessity of calling back later, when the door to number 86, the next door up the corridor, abruptly opened.

A girl's head popped out. Her face was young, slightly freckled, but pretty with a warm, generous mouth. Her dark hair was wet, and the brief glimpse of the rest of her, mostly hidden behind the door, was wrapped in a large blue bath towel.

'You looking for Mike?'

Falcon nodded.

'He's not in. I mean he's in town, but he's not in the apartment.' She smiled at her own confusion. 'You're lucky really, most of the time he's out at the Game Park, but this is one of the weekends when he comes back to Jo'burg to beer up and paint the town.' She paused. 'Can I tell him who called?'

Falcon decided he didn't want Kyller forewarned. He said gently, 'Perhaps you can tell me where I can find Mike?'

The girl stopped exchanging smiles and pouted her mouth. She didn't look quite so pretty then, and Falcon knew she had been sulking.

'You might find him at the Golden Crescent. It's a downtown bar. That's where he usually drinks.'

'Thank you,' Falcon said. 'I'll look there for him.' He smiled at her again, raised a hand in parting and turned away.

The girl looked depressed, as though she had lost two games in a row. She obviously knew Kyller well and did not approve of his solo drinking habits.

'If you find him,' she called after Falcon somewhat bitterly. 'You can tell him that Judy was looking for him too.'

CHAPTER 3

The Golden Crescent was the Witwatersrand Reef, the vast, rich quarter moon of gold seams buried deep in the earth, and spreading out for many miles on either side of the city. In daylight mountainous excavations of bright yellow earth blended with the modern high-rise blocks, monuments and towers, to form Johannesburg's unique skyline; while more than a mile deep below its pavements near-naked black Africans still sweated over their hammering drills in the mines.

By night and by contrast the bar which bore the same name could have been located anywhere. It was one of the more dimly lit establishments among the bright blaze of discotheques, coffee bars and nightclubs of Hillbrow, not too far from the tower block apartment.

Falcon's taxi-driver found the place quickly and easily and deposited him on the pavement. He stood for a moment, taking stock of the area, and decided that his own preference would have been for one of the more swinging places generating sounds of music further down the street.

It was a basement bar and he descended a flight of steps to pass through trailing curtains of bright glass beads. The room beyond was smoke-filled and crowded, mostly with male drinkers. It plainly catered more for serious beer consumption than for champagne-spiced entertainment.

His eyes accustomed quickly to the gloom, and when he moved up to the bar he couldn't help noticing the young blonde woman seated in the far corner on a leather-topped stool. She was noticeable for a variety of reasons. She was beautiful. Her face was partially turned away from him, but her hair was a wave of soft gold. She was poised, cool and elegant. And she was alone.

There were men looking at her but she did not seem to notice. She did not look like the usual bar pick-up, and at any other time Falcon might have been intrigued. Tonight he was not.

He ordered a cold beer, which was what most of the men here were drinking, and then half turned with his back to the bar. He scanned the room casually, looking for Mike Kyller.

He saw the ex-mercenary almost immediately. Kyller was sitting at a small table with his back to the wall. He was a big man of about forty-five with black hair and a hard, suntanned face. Above his right eye was a small pucker of scar tissue from an old bullet crease.

Kyller was alone, one elbow on the table, his chin cupped in his hand as he stared vacantly into an almost empty beer glass. He looked like a man with something heavy on his mind.

Falcon turned back to the bar, paid for his beer, and drank slowly. He waited until he was sure that no one else was going to join Kyller, then he pretended to notice the man for the first time.

He walked over, smiling cheerfully. 'Hello! It's Sergeant Kyller, I do believe. I often wondered what had happened to you?'

Kyller looked up, blankly. He had been drinking heavily and there was no recognition in his eyes.

'We met in Angola,' Falcon reminded him. 'Beside an armoured car on a bush road in the middle of nowhere. You were just about to tell me the story of your life, when a MiG-21 broke up the party.'

'Angola,' Kyller repeated slowly. He had to think hard, but then his weathered features split into a grin. 'Hey, man, you were with a newspaper, or something.'

'*Empire News Service,*' Falcon admitted. 'I wrote a big feature on the Angola war. It got printed in a lot of magazines. Your name got a mention, even though I never did finish talking to you.'

'Hell, man, I thought you must be dead. You were leaning right up against that truck when that MiG put a rocket up its arse. I figured you roasted in that little fireball for sure.'

Falcon smiled. 'I dived clear. I lost my camera, my notebook and my ballpoint — but when I finished rolling at least I still had my boots on and my skin.'

'So you got out. I'm glad you made it. Our troop scattered to the four winds, and when that bastard in the MiG came back in a strafing run with his canon we just kept on going.'

His smile became rueful and he shrugged his shoulders. 'Sorry we left you, but it didn't seem worth the risk to go back just to pick up the pieces. The bloody ruskies were pouring fighters and tanks and helicopters into Angola, so our war was pretty much a hit-and-run effort. And most of it was bloody running.'

'No hard feelings,' Falcon assured him. 'I knew the score.'

Kyller grinned, and abruptly swallowed the last mouthful of beer from his glass. 'This is worth another drink. Have one with me?'

'I was going to buy you one.'

'My first shout,' Kyller insisted. 'I owe you.'

He took his empty glass up to the bar and came back with two full pints. He had cheered up at the prospect of reliving the old war and his eyes gleamed with returning memories. He sat down and raised his glass.

'Here's to you, Mister—?'

'Falcon. Mark Falcon.'

'Yank?'

'No. English.'

'Well, whatever you are, you must have walked two hundred miles or more to find us that time, so you must be okay.'

Falcon smiled, and raised his own glass. 'Thanks, Sergeant.'

'That was six years ago. No rank now. Just plain Mike Kyller.'

'So you finished after Angola?'

Kyller shrugged. 'Angola was a bloody mess, man. It wasn't like the other wars. When Moscow took over and all the bloody Cubans flooded in to support the MPLA, then that was the end. Besides, mercenaries got a bad name in Angola. That stupid bloody Colonel Callan in the north, and those green English kids who came out with him. They were nothing to do with us, but Callan's dead and the ones who didn't die are still rotting in Luanda jail. They weren't old hands. Most of them had never seen Africa before. But they got all the publicity.'

'The north was a mess,' Falcon agreed tactfully. He could see that Kyller could easily turn sour and ugly and he didn't want the other man to become bitter. 'For my money UNITA was the only real contender.'

'UNITA had half the country behind them. The Marxists only had a quarter and the shambles in the north had the other quarter. In any kind of straight fight or free election UNITA would have won. But Russia and Cuba made sure they didn't.'

Kyller looked as though he wanted to spit in disgust, then he shrugged his shoulders. 'Anyway, it taught me a lesson. There was no more future for a mercenary in Africa, not on the ground anyway. I took my pay from that last campaign, and just for once I didn't piss it up the wall. I bought flying lessons. I'm a pilot now, man. I fly helicopters.'

'Sounds like a good investment.'

'Sure thing. At first I figured I'd fly to the next war. But then I figured why be dumb all my life. A MiG would shoot the arse off a helicopter in no time. So I went civilian. I've got a partner now. A guy named Jacobsen.' He paused, looking shrewdly at Falcon. 'You on vacation, still working for that newspaper, or what?'

'A bit of both,' Falcon said casually. 'Mostly vacation.'

'Then why don't you come up to the Kruger Game Park. I'll be back there in a couple of days. Me and Jacobsen, we fly helicopter photographic safaris. I'll take you on a cut-rate trip. You bring your camera. If you've got a telephoto lens, then I can promise you the best wildlife pictures you'll ever get. Impala, lion, leopard, elephant — we've got it all up at Kruger.'

Falcon let him talk, throwing a question here and there just to keep the conversation flowing. Kyller relaxed again, telling big game stories and describing the thrills of flying low along the twisting courses of the Limpopo and Crocodile rivers.

Finally Falcon decided it was time to try and turn the conversation back to where he wanted it. He waited until Kyller stopped to drink more of his beer, and then said: 'It sounds an exciting life.' He tapped a finger to his right temple. 'And better than getting shot at.'

Kyller grinned. For a moment his hand strayed up to touch the small bullet scar above his own right eye.

'Yeah, man. This one is from the Congo, back in sixty-four. Now that was a war where a mercenary commando could really do a good job. The Simbas were butchering nuns and missionaries left, right and centre. We saw some bloody grim sights in the Congo, but we made some good rescues too. We were all heroes then. The press was on our side.'

'I covered the Congo war too. I followed Hoare and Five Commando into Stanleyville.'

This time Falcon lied, because in 1964 he had been fighting his own war in Borneo at the beginning of his career with the SAS. But it was a safe lie, because what had been the Belgian Congo was a vast area of over 900,000 square miles. There was plenty of room for two men to miss each other and Falcon's pre-mission checks had shown that Kyller had not fought anywhere near the town of Stanleyville.

However, he wanted to keep the conversation on an equal footing, to sound familiar with Kyller's world. He went on casually:

'You were with Nine Commando. They did some good work. I seem to remember that you were teamed up with a black sergeant — an extraordinary character — I think he was the only black African mercenary I've ever met.'

Kyller's smile faded slowly. His body tensed and his face froze.

It was too late to turn back. Falcon frowned into his beer, as though unaware of Kyller's reaction and struggling to remember the name.

'Katanga. No — that was the province down south where they had the first rebellion. But something like that. Kataka? No — Kitaka. That's it, Jonas Kitaka.'

Falcon looked up again at Kyller. 'Whatever happened to him?'

'I don't know, man.' Kyller's voice was hoarse. His eyes were ugly. 'That was a long time ago. Why should I know?'

Falcon shrugged his shoulders. 'No reason, except that I've heard his name again just recently. I thought he was something of a celebrity in this part of the world, one of the new guerrilla leaders.'

'Is that why you came here? To ask me about Jonas Kitaka?'

'Of course not.' Falcon looked startled by the threatening tone. 'I thought we were just talking over old wars — old faces.'

Kyller was rigid with suspicion, staring into Falcon's face with beer-dulled eyes, searching for any hint of duplicity.

'Then talk about something else, man. You hear me? Don't talk about that bastard.'

'Okay.' Falcon spread his hands defensively. 'Okay.'

Kyller scowled, and then slumped moodily over his empty glass. Falcon waited a minute and then tried to retrieve the situation. He reached for the empty glasses.

'We're out of beer. I'll get some more.'

'Wait a minute.' Kyller's hand locked in a hard grip on his arm. The hot, angry eyes stared again at Falcon. 'I want to know what this is all about? Did you come all the way to South Africa just to ask me about Jonas Kitaka.'

'No,' Falcon tried to calm him. 'I just want to buy you a drink.'

'Look, man, I don't know anything about Kitaka. I haven't seen him in fifteen years.'

'Okay, I believe you.'

'Like hell you do.' Kyller lurched to his feet, the drink and suspicion fermenting into sudden rage inside him. 'You know something, man. You want something. What is it?'

'Cool it, Mike. I thought we were friends.'

'No, man — not anymore.' Kyller's left hand was still locked on Falcon's arm. His right hand scooped up one of the empty glasses and smashed it on the edge of the table. 'You're gonna tell me, man. Or I'm gonna carve it out of you.'

Falcon eased up on to his feet, balanced and ready, the old instincts of unarmed combat training flowing smoothly through his mind and muscles.

'Put the glass down, Mike. You're making a mistake.'

'Tell me!' Kyller roared, and the jagged edge of the broken beer glass jabbed to within an inch of Falcon's left eye.

Falcon's head weaved neatly just out of reach and his free hand caught the wrist of the hand that held the glass. For a moment they pitted their strength against each other.

'Mike—' Falcon tried once more but it was no use.

Kyller gave another bellow of drunken fury, jerked himself back to break free, and then made another wild, slashing forward lunge with the broken glass.

Falcon had been trained in every aspect of armed and unarmed combat. The S.A.S. had turned him into the ultimate soldier, a reflex killing machine, but still an intelligent thinking man with a high code of honour. He could — and had — killed when necessity demanded, always swiftly, mercifully, and without undue remorse. In any fighting situation he was fast, sharp and deadly.

He had to defend himself, but he didn't want to kill Mike Kyller. Again he sidestepped the thrust of the broken glass that was aiming to rip his throat out, catching Kyller's wrist in both hands, twisting and turning the South African over the pivot of his own hip. Kyller crashed down bodily to the floor.

The ex-mercenary was tough. He clambered up again with surprising speed, still clutching the broken glass and seeming to sober with the action. He turned and lunged again, but Falcon had picked up the table and was using it as a shield.

The jagged edge embedded deep in the tabletop and Kyller howled as the glass shattered completely and gashed open his own fingers. He shook away the splinters and bright droplets of red blood, and then came forward with balled fists.

Falcon tossed the table to one side and hit him three times. One to the heart to stop him in his tracks, one to the stomach to double him up, and a sharp palm chop to the neck to tumble him unconscious back to the floor. The three blows all blurred into one continuous stream of motion.

The room had been shocked into silence. Falcon breathed deeply twice and then turned to the bar. He dropped three ten rand banknotes on the counter and gave the bartender an apologetic smile.

'We're good friends really. It's just the drink in him. I hope that takes care of the damage.'

The bartender nodded. He was too startled to argue.

'Then I'll get him out,' Falcon offered. 'I'll take him home.'

He turned back to Kyller, lifting the unconscious man up and propping him against the bar counter for a moment. He dropped to one knee and pulled Kyller smoothly across his shoulders. He straightened up again, and while most of the bar customers were still gaping he carried his burden easily up the exit steps and out on to the street.

He paused and looked for a taxi, hoping to get Kyller away quickly before there were any more complications. There were none in sight and he began to walk.

Two minutes later a sleek, black Lancia sports car eased up from behind him. It was an open top, and at the wheel he recognized the ice-cool blonde who had been sitting at the bar.

'There was another bartender at my end,' she informed him calmly. 'I heard him telephone the police while you were still fighting. So maybe you'd best climb in and throw him in the back.'

Her smile was frank and inviting.

Falcon hesitated for a moment, but then he heard the wail of an approaching siren. His options were limited and with a word of thanks he accepted the offer and the advice.

His unexpected ally shifted the gearstick, put her foot hard down on the accelerator and drove on without a backward glance. She was still smiling, and looked as though she was enjoying herself.

CHAPTER 4

Kyller had to know something about the present activities of Jonas Kitaka. Falcon was sure of this much from Kyller's violent reaction to the mere mention of the terrorist leader's name. No man flew into an immediate rage over a name that no longer had any meaning.

So Falcon hoped that it was still possible to salvage something from the situation. In fact, finding Kyller drunk might eventually prove to have been an advantage. Sober the ex-mercenary would have been more careful, guarding his words and his reactions, but the combination of drink, fear and temper had betrayed him.

Fear was the key word. After his sojourn in Borneo, and in other equally dangerous parts of the world, Falcon had learned to recognize the smell of fear. And Kyller had been afraid — drunk and angry, but most of all, afraid.

Obviously Kyller would not want to be involved with the police, and so by getting him out of the Golden Crescent fast, before the police could arrive, Falcon hoped to earn some measure of the man's thanks. He was trying to put himself in the best position to win some real information from Kyller when the South African had had time to sober up.

All these calculations were weighed in his mind as the Lancia made the short journey back to Kyller's apartment block. The blonde woman had asked, 'Where to?' And after he had given her the address she had kept her attention on the road. She stayed silent, still half smiling, and handled the car and the situation with skill and confidence.

When they arrived she switched off the ignition and half turned to face him. Her eyes were summer-sky blue. Her face was strong but well shaped. Falcon guessed she was Dutch Afrikaans, a great-granddaughter of one of the tough old Boer families that had trekked north from the Cape to found the Orange Free State and the Transvaal a hundred-and-fifty years before.

'He's a big man, and he's a dead weight.' With a toss of her head she indicated Kyller slumped in the back of the car. 'I'd best go ahead of you and open doors and things.'

She had been an invaluable help and there was no way he could refuse. She waved away his thanks and helped him to get Kyller back on to his shoulders. Then, as good as her word, she walked ahead to open the hall door and call down the elevator.

He gave her the floor number and she pressed the button. As they travelled upward they were pressed closer together than they had been in the car, and again he was aware that this was a very beautiful woman.

'I'm getting deeper in your debt,' he said. 'And I still don't know your name?'

'Helen Collier,' she told him. 'And you?'

'Mark Falcon.'

'Hello.' She grinned and nudged Kyller. 'Him you can introduce later. If he ever wakes up.'

They reached the eighth floor and he led the way down the corridor to number 87. There he stopped with Kyller still draped over his shoulders.

'Try his pockets,' he suggested. 'We might find his keys.'

Helen obliged, feeling in the breast pocket of Kyller's bush shirt, and then trying to get her fingers into the deep pockets of his trousers. However, before she could find anything, the door to number 86 flew open.

The face of the girl Judy appeared again. She was dressed now in a blue T-shirt and jeans, and Falcon guessed she had been listening for Kyller's return. She came out into the corridor, her eyes wide with alarm.

'Oh, my God. Mike! What's happened?'

'He's had a couple of beers.' Falcon spoke quietly to calm her. 'He fell and hit his head, but he's only knocked himself out. I thought I'd best bring him home.'

'Oh, Mike.' She lifted his head to look into his face, biting her lip for a moment before she looked back anxiously to Falcon. 'Bring him into my place,' she offered. 'I'll look after him.'

Falcon had the feeling that he was being besieged by too many, too-helpful women, but again it was an offer difficult to refuse. He hesitated for a moment and then allowed Judy to lead him into her apartment. There was a studio couch in the main living room and he lowered Kyller on to it. Judy fussed round the man, putting cushions beneath his head.

Falcon checked Kyller over. The South African was breathing harshly but steadily, and appeared to have taken no real harm in the fight. Judy moaned to her maker again when she saw the blood on Kyller's fingers.

'He broke a glass,' Falcon explained. 'The cuts just need bathing and taping up with some sticking plaster.'

'I can do it. I'll take care of him.' The freckle-faced girl seemed pathetically eager to help the drunken man who didn't seem to deserve her lip-biting concern.

'Thanks.' Falcon decided that Kyller probably wouldn't sober up until the next morning, so there was little more he could do here now. He could safely leave Kyller to Judy.

'When Mike comes round you can tell him I'll call him sometime tomorrow,' he told her. 'Tell him there's no hard feelings, and that I still owe him a beer.'

'I'll tell him.' Judy looked up uncertainly. 'He doesn't usually get like this. Thank you for bringing him home.'

'It's okay.' Falcon smiled at her as he backed out. 'I'll see you again,' he promised as he closed the door.

Helen Collier was waiting for him outside. She linked her arm with his and smiled cheerfully as they walked back to the elevator.

'Well, champ, where do we go from here?'

Falcon accepted a lift back to his hotel and invited her into the lounge bar for a drink. The atmosphere here was quiet, plush luxury. It was a whole world away from the Golden Crescent, a bright new world of gilt-edged mirrors, silver chandeliers and thick pile carpet. And no one was drinking beer.

Helen chose a gin and tonic, Falcon a whisky with ice, and they moved with the drinks to the relative privacy of a small table in the far corner of the large room. They relaxed into comfortable red velvet armchairs and toasted each other.

'I know I shouldn't look a gift horse in the mouth,' Falcon said casually. 'But I can't help wondering why?'

'Why I helped you?' Helen laughed softly. 'Perhaps I'm your guardian angel.'

Falcon smiled and made a negative movement of his head. 'I would like to believe you, but angels have wings.'

'So look to your right.'

Falcon turned his head, and saw his own reflection in one of the full length, gilt-framed mirrors.

'Now you see what I see. A very handsome man. I just go for hazel eyes and dark blond hair. And when you look like a film star, and go into action like the perfect fighting machine, then you shouldn't be surprised when women get interested.'

'Thanks for all the flattery.' Falcon smiled again. 'I could say just as many nice things about you, and they would be even more true. But you are not just a spoiled rich girl looking for kicks with any interesting man.'

'Thank you, but what makes you so sure?'

Falcon shrugged. 'The car, your expensive clothes, all suggest a comfortable background. A sophisticated young woman, yes. But idle, bored, looking for any excitement — definitely no. You have a certain self-assurance. You know where you are going.'

He leaned forward and looked deep in her eyes. 'Try me again.'

'Okay, okay — you win!' She put up her hands in mock surrender. 'I admit it, Mark. I recognized you. And when I saw a famous international news correspondent talking to an ex-mercenary, then I naturally got curious.'

'Why naturally?'

'Because we have the same instincts. We're in the same business. I'm a reporter with the *Rand Daily Mail*. A couple of years ago I was their London correspondent. That's when you were pointed out to me, in a Fleet Street pub, although it was crowded at the time and I didn't get close enough to get introduced. When I saw you again and realized who you were, I scented a story.'

This time it sounded credible. Falcon watched her face and decided he believed her.

Helen leaned forward. 'So now it's my turn to ask the questions. What is the story, Mark? Why did you come all the way to South Africa just to talk to Mike Kyller?'

Falcon shrugged. 'I'm sorry, but there isn't a story. I just met Kyller by chance. I interviewed him once in Angola. What we were reliving was dead news.'

Helen looked disappointed, and disbelieving. 'So why did you come to Johannesburg?'

'For a vacation.' Falcon knew that wasn't enough and added a grain of truth. 'In a couple of weeks I'm going to cover the Project *Vulcan* rocket launch in Mozambique. I figured in the meantime I could see a bit more of Africa, and put all the travelling down to my legitimate expenses.'

'Hey!' Her smile flashed. 'I'm covering *Vulcan* too. They only invited one South African reporter. The paper they chose was the *Mail* — and the *Mail* chose me.'

'So we shall meet again in Mozambique.' Falcon raised his glass. 'It looks as though we now have two good reasons to get acquainted.'

They finished the drinks and Falcon ordered two more. While they waited Helen gave him her direct, questioning look.

'I still don't believe you about Mike Kyller,' she told him bluntly. 'I heard you asking him about Jonas Kitaka?'

'A chance question to follow a chance meeting,' Falcon returned blandly. 'Kitaka's been in the news recently, and I remembered that he and Kyller once fought together in the Congo. Like you I have a nose for a story — and I guess that like yours it doesn't always lead me where I want to go.'

'If you go after Kitaka, you go after trouble,' she warned him seriously. 'That man is bad. He's the worst, or the best, of the terrorist leaders. It depends on your point of view.'

'And what's your point of view?'

'I knew it was coming.' This time her smile was bitter. 'When a South African meets an American or a European we always get the same question, but always full of implied righteousness and criticism.'

'Perhaps I shouldn't have asked.'

'No, it's best to get it over. The simple answer is that I was born into the white tribe of Africa. I can understand the black tribes wanting to improve their way of life, but I don't want to see my way of life destroyed. For us the population statistics don't count. This land was empty when our forefathers first explored it. Everything that is here now the whites have created. We belong here and we have nowhere else to go. How can you say that we are wrong?'

'And how can you say that apartheid is right?'

'I can't, and I won't. But what is right for one tribe is always wrong for another. That's history. If apartheid fails we disappear, like the Greeks, the Romans, and the British Empire.'

'Apartheid must fail, eventually.'

'Then men like Kitaka will take over, and you'll all see what you piously pretend you don't want — another Congo, an Angola, or a Uganda.'

'Do you really think Kitaka has that big a following?'

'He's big enough. He's hitting us where it hurts. Yesterday the oil refineries, today the power stations. In black eyes that makes him a big hero. They forget that so far he's killed more blacks than whites to get where he is today.'

She paused, giving him the direct look again. 'Did you get anything out of Mike Kyller?'

'Nothing. He said he hadn't seen Kitaka in fifteen years.'

'And you believed him?'

'Why shouldn't I?' Falcon matched her searching stare. 'Why are you so interested? How much do you know about Jonas Kitaka?'

'Only as much as any one in South Africa knows.'

'Do you know where he is now?'

'He could be anywhere — in South Africa, or over the borders in Zimbabwe or Mozambique. Nobody knows.'

She was silent for a moment, frowning a little, and Falcon knew that it was time to change the subject.

'Let's forget politics,' he suggested. 'Tell me more about Helen Collier.'

While Falcon and Helen Collier were cementing their new friendship, Mike Kyller was struggling slowly back to consciousness. He blinked open his eyes and saw the worried face of Judy hovering over him.

With an effort he struggled up, recognizing the room, and remembering what had happened. The top of his head throbbed with a familiar hangover, while the back of his neck hurt with a less familiar but equally insidious ache. It all made thinking difficult.

'How did I get here?' he muttered miserably.

'Your friend brought you home,' Judy told him. 'He said you had a fall and hit your head. I brought you in here. Mike, you've cut your fingers. What happened?'

'Friend?' Kyller demanded curtly. 'What friend?'

'The tall blond man. I don't know his name. He was here earlier. He said he would come back tomorrow.' She blurted the words quickly, trying to speed them out of the way so she could ask her own questions. 'Mike, who was he? What did he want?'

Kyller ignored her, he was trying to concentrate. Falcon had been looking for him earlier in the evening, so their meeting in the bar had nothing to do with chance. Falcon had also brought him home, despite their fight, and intended to see him again. It all added up to a lot of persistence. Falcon knew something. Or was after something.

'Oh, Christ,' Kyller groaned. He tried desperately to remember every word that had passed between them.

'What is it, Mike?' Judy sat on the couch beside him, putting one slim arm around his shoulders.'

'Leave it,' Kyller snapped rudely. He pushed her away and stood up, stumbling as he headed for the door. 'I gotta call somebody.'

'Mike, stay here. Use my phone. You're not fit—'

Kyller slammed the door in her face. She stared at it, helpless, hurt and humiliated, and for the moment too shocked even to cry.

Kyller fumbled for his key and let himself into his own apartment next door. He closed the door behind him and deliberately locked it again, just in case Judy tried to follow him. The call he had to make had to be private, and he stumbled to the telephone and dialled a number.

Within two minutes he was talking to Jonas Kitaka.

'This guy is bad trouble,' he finished on a note of panic. 'He wanted to know about you, Jonas. He's on to something.'

'Stay cool, man,' the deep, cautious voice advised. 'Don't go losing your stupid white head.'

'But what about tomorrow night? If this guy Falcon is still trailing at my heels—?'

Kitaka thought for a moment. 'Okay, man, if this guy wants to play your puppy dog then let him follow. Give him an invite. Just make sure you come to the meeting place like we arranged. If you're being stalked, we'll make sure he ends up dead.'

'Jonas, he's a newspaperman. Killing him could stir up a lot of trouble.'

'In a few days it won't matter.'

'It'll matter to me. His people will know I'm involved.'

'Sergeant Mike,' the deep voice oozed with menace. 'You got two choices. You do what I tell you, or I make sure our little Congo secret gets to the newspapers. And right now I'm telling you to make sure this guy follows you tomorrow night.'

Kyller's knuckles were white where he gripped the telephone, and the veins stood out taut on his neck. He felt sick in his stomach, as though he wanted to vomit up all the stale beer, frustration and anger.

'Do it right,' Kitaka warned, and hung up.

CHAPTER 5

The night air was sweet and cool where the road climbed east into the Vumba Mountains. A few miles ahead was the border town of Umtali, with beyond a steep ascent through the high forest to the border itself, and then a drop of thousands of feet to the vast Mozambique plain.

A white Toyota car had pulled up on one side of the road. Inside were three men. Two of them were black Africans. The third, no longer in uniform, but wearing a nondescript dark T-shirt and trousers like his companions, was Salem Sharif.

The man who called himself Jeremiah leaned back from the wheel and flexed his shoulder muscles. It was a two-hour drive from Salisbury, the capital of Zimbabwe, and Jeremiah had been hunched over the wheel and silent throughout the journey. Now he looked behind him and spoke.

'You must cross the border on foot. From here Samson will guide you. He knows the border country well.'

Samson had been equally uncommunicative since the brief, grunted introductions when they had first met. He turned his head and nodded briefly. 'He is right. We walk.'

Sharif was tempted to argue. He could see no reason why they should not simply drive on through Umtali, and save a few miles of foot-slogging to bypass the town. Then he guessed that Samson would have his own favourite forest trails — the terrorist infiltration routes he had learned by heart when Zimbabwe was still Rhodesia. Sharif wanted to tell them that particular guerrilla war was over, but then he decided it would be best to let them do things in their own way. He was a guest, and he had to be discreet.

'Very well.' He nodded agreement.

He hesitated for a moment, but Jeremiah made no move to shake hands or to wish him luck. The black man had approached Sharif in the hotel where he had stayed in Salisbury, making contact as had been arranged. But he had not been friendly. He had no knowledge of Sharif's final purpose, and resented the fact that he had been kept ignorant. He had stayed aloof, and now his job was done.

'Goodbye,' Sharif said, keeping his face impassive. 'Thank you for your help.'

Jeremiah shrugged. Sharif got out of the car.

Samson got out and pointed north-east, away from the road, into the wooded hills.

'This way,' he instructed, and began to walk with long, fast strides.

Sharif shouldered his rucksack and followed without looking back. He heard the car start up and turn around to begin the journey back to Salisbury.

Samson and Jeremiah, both good Christian Bible names, Sharif thought briefly. And he wondered how many bewildered missionaries the two ex-guerrillas had chopped up between their schooldays and their country's hard-won independence.

An hour later they were moving up a steep forest trail. Insects clamoured in the thick darkness, and unseen leaves and tangles of foliage constantly brushed Sharif's body and face. He had to stay close to Samson's heels or he would have lost his guide in the night, and only occasionally did the African glance round to see if he was still there.

Not one word had passed between them. Samson was as silent and distant as Jeremiah had been.

It was then that Sharif began to feel uneasy.

Perhaps it was the claustrophobic atmosphere of the black forest, so alien to the empty deserts of his northern homeland. Or perhaps it was because he was beginning to place a new interpretation on the reticence of his African allies.

Suddenly he realized that their aloofness was not necessarily resentment, but might merely be a simple reluctance to extend a wasted hand of friendship. They were treating him like a man who was not expected to return alive from his mission.

It was ten o'clock the following morning when the telephone rang in Falcon's hotel room. He came out of the bathroom with a towel round his waist to answer it. He was expecting to hear the desk clerk enquire whether he wanted to order breakfast, and was surprised to hear instead the harsh but hesitant voice of Mike Kyller.

'Mark, is that you, man? I owe you an apology for last night.'

'Mike, it's okay. Like I told your girl friend — there's no hard feelings.'

'I still feel bad, man. I just don't know what the hell got into me. I know I have a lousy temper — and I guess last night I had too much to drink.'

'It's okay,' Falcon repeated. He frowned and asked cautiously, 'How did you know where to find me?'

'I called a few of the big hotels. This was the fourth.' Kyller sounded awkward. Apologies were not his style. 'I guess I got to thank you for getting me out of that place last night.'

'It was the least I could do.' Falcon wondered what Kyller was leading up to. 'I was the one who hit you.'

'Yeah, I got the bruise. What the hell were we arguing about?'

'I'm not really sure.' Falcon waited, but Kyller seemed to be stuck for words and after a moment he had to help the man out. 'We were talking about an old friend of yours. Jonas Kitaka. The name seemed to make you mad.'

'Sure. That's it. I got a lot of hate for that bastard. On our last campaign in the Congo he chickened out of a Simba attack. I led our troop into an ambush. Jonas was rearguard. He backed out and left me for dead.'

'It happens,' Falcon murmured wryly. He was thinking of Angola but decided it would be tactless to spell it out.

'Except that I wasn't dead and Jonas knew it.' Kyller didn't seem to hear Falcon's remark and charged on. 'Those Simbas would have cut my balls off and made me eat them. But Jonas didn't care. He ran out on me. I was lucky to get away from that one alive — and no thanks to Sergeant Kitaka.'

'That's a big enough grievance for any man.' Falcon didn't believe a word of it but he pretended sympathy.

'Yeah.' Kyller stalled again. It sounded as though he was swallowing something solid, like his self-respect. He was finding the conversation difficult but he pushed on. 'Mark, are you really looking for Kitaka?'

'He's news, Mike, and I'm always looking for a story.' Falcon understood now and waited for the proposition.

'He's bad trouble, but I loathe his guts and I owe you for last night.' Kyller paused again, then tried to make the sell-out sound more convincing. 'There's a lot of risk in this for me, Mark. But I need some hard cash and I need it fast. If I do give you a lead to Kitaka, then how much would your newspaper pay for that kind of information?'

Falcon allowed half a minute to pass, as though he needed to think. 'Five hundred US dollars,' he offered at last.

'Christ, man, it must be worth at least five thousand!'

'One thousand if the lead is really hot.' It was Falcon's turn to sound apologetic, although they both knew they were playing a game. 'That's as high as ENS will allow me to go.'

'Okay.' Kyller agreed too readily. Then he added a hasty cover-up. 'But only because I want to even a score.'

'Then we have a deal. What's the information?'

Kyller drew a deep breath, and the carefully rehearsed words flowed smoothly over the telephone. 'I know this man who swears he knows where to find Kitaka. He was a member of *Black K*, but somehow Jonas played dirty with him too. He's got his own grudge, and he wants to see Jonas caught. I've been planning to use him to set Jonas up. I was gonna sell Jonas to the police — there's a reward on his head — but because I owe you I'll let you get to him first.'

'What's the name of this man?'

'Temela.' The hesitation was only momentary. Kyller had said the first name to come into his head.

'So how are you going to set up Jonas Kitaka?'

'I haven't figured out all the details yet, and even if I had I couldn't talk over the phone. But I've got a meeting with Temela tonight. He's going to take me into Soweto, that's the black township outside Jo'burg. He'll shy off if he sees you with me. But if you want to take a chance and follow me out there — keep your distance and stay back out of sight until I call you — then maybe I can persuade him to talk to you.'

'And you think Temela can lead us to Kitaka?'

'He can make contact. And Jonas just might talk to you for publicity, to get his views printed. He'd take that kind of bait. We let you talk first, then we spring a police trap.'

'It sounds good.' Falcon knew that Kyller was now making it up as they went along. 'But we have to meet somewhere, Mike, to talk this over. Name a bar and I'll buy you that beer.'

'No.' Kyller blurted in panic. 'I'm gonna be busy all day today. But I'll be leaving my place to drive to Soweto at ten-thirty tonight. I'll be in a yellow Land Rover, short wheelbase, a bit beat-up.'

'I'll call at your apartment—'

'Don't do that. I might be watched. Just follow me, and stay well back until I get a chance to talk to Temela. If he sees you too soon he'll cut and run. That'll screw up everything. Let me talk to him first.'

'Okay,' Falcon agreed. 'We'll do it your way.'

'Yeah, sure, I'll see you later.' There was a click and the line went dead.

Falcon replaced his receiver slowly, and for almost a minute he stood deep in silent thought.

'It's a trap,' Helen Collier volunteered at last.

She was lying naked in his bed, a single sheet drawn up just above the level of her hips. He had almost forgotten that she was there, but now he realized that her ears were sharp enough to have overheard the whole of his conversation with Kyller.

'I know,' he admitted.

'The name he mentioned — Temela — that's Nicholas Temela. He's Number Two in the *Black K* organization, Jonas Kitaka's right-hand man. He wouldn't betray Kitaka.'

Falcon smiled. 'It gets more interesting.'

'It stinks, Mark. You can't go.'

'But I am going. If I let this pass up, Kyller will disappear. That will be the end of it.'

'Is that so important? Why is this story worth your life?'

'No special reason, but in one way or another I risk my life on every other story I write. It's an occupational hazard.'

She shifted up on to one elbow, giving him her candid eye-to-eye stare. 'You mean it, don't you? Well, if you're that determined, then I'm coming too.'

'No,' he said firmly. 'That's out.'

'You'd be a fool to go without me. I know this country and I know its people. I speak Afrikaans and a smattering of Zulu and Xhosa. I have a fast car and I know Jo'burg like the back of my hand. You could run into all kinds of unnecessary problems without me.'

'And you could run into some unnecessary problems by coming with me.'

'I'll take that chance.' She smiled softly. 'You're something special, Mark. I don't tumble straight into bed with every man on the first night we meet. Usually it takes quite a long time. That should tell you just how special and irresistible you are. You're a once-in-a-lifetime find, and I don't intend to lose you just as quickly.'

Falcon looked her over with approval. Their love-making had been unbelievably good for such a short relationship. She had a lively and intelligent mind and the physical attraction had been mutual. He was sure that neither of them had expected to jump into the same bed so quickly, and yet it had happened easily and naturally because they had both sensed that they would enjoy each other.

'You're a rare discovery, yourself,' he assured her.

Helen's eyes softened. She laid back on the bed and reached one hand to pull at the knot holding the towel round his waist. As the towel dropped to the floor she raised up her left knee and lazily pushed back the sheet that was her only covering.

'We've got plenty of time,' she pointed out. 'A whole day to fill. Let's start at the beginning and do last night all over again.'

CHAPTER 6

At ten o'clock the black Lancia sports car was parked in a side street where they could watch the exit from the underground car park below Kyller's apartment block. Helen was at the wheel, wearing a dark blue jumper and skirt, and a black silk scarf masking her blonde hair. Falcon was beside her, also dressed in dark clothing, suitable for night work.

Falcon had his arm around her shoulders and they talked quietly. To anyone passing by they looked like any ordinary courting couple. They waited for thirty minutes, and then Kyller's battered Land Rover appeared dead on time, nosing up slowly from the underground ramp and turning away from them down the street.

'That must be it,' Falcon decided. He couldn't see the driver's face, but the vehicle description fitted.

Helen nodded and started the engine of the Lancia. Holding back as far as they dared they followed the Land Rover out of the busy city centre. They were heading due west, and Falcon noted road signs for Roodepoort and Krugersdorp.

Kyller was driving carefully, making it easy for them to keep him in sight. After some five or six miles he turned south off the main road, and abruptly the bright lights and the concrete canyons were behind them. They were driving through the open fields which separated the white city from the black township.

Helen let the Lancia fall even further behind, until the tail lights of the Land Rover were just faint red pinpricks in the darkness ahead.

Behind them was the violet night glow of Johannesburg. Ahead for a while there was nothing, and then a few low level glimmers of yellow light. Johannesburg was a blaze of neon glory, comparable to New York or London, but in Soweto only a third of the houses had electricity. The rest made do with oil lamps and candles.

Falcon knew that Soweto stood for South Western Townships, and that it extended over 34 square miles. It contained over a million inhabitants, many of whom travelled by train to spend their working days in Johannesburg, but were obliged to return on the same trains every evening to spend the night in their own mean ghetto.

This sprawling black satellite, deliberately separated from the white capital, was also the focus of everything that was wrong in South Africa. It was a vast human stain of racial anger and tensions, which had exploded frequently into violence and confrontation against the ruling whites.

Helen seemed to read his thoughts. She said calmly, 'You can compare what's ahead to Jo'burg, or you can compare it to the mud huts that form most African villages north of the Limpopo. We've built a different world down here. And we're the villains for it.'

'You could try sharing it.'

'With the Bantu? To you that sounds reasonable. But it's easy to argue statistics and morality when you don't have to live here.' Her voice became bitter for a moment. 'Perhaps we should have done what the Americans did with their natives — killed off the warriors in a series of wars, and herded the rest on to reservations way back in the eighteenth century when the rest of the world wasn't looking. We're paying now for past mistakes.'

'And present mistakes. Apartheid is the biggest mistake of all.'

'We know.' The bitterness became weariness. 'But we're on a road of no return. Your Western newspapers accuse us of having a laager mentality, and in a sense its true. We are in laager. We're on the defensive with apartheid replacing the circle of ox-waggons around us, and outside the Zulu hordes fighting to get in. We've only got until the laager breaks, and then we'll be destroyed, but we see no point in breaking the laager ourselves.'

'There must be another way.'

'Maybe there is, Mark. Maybe you can see one. Perhaps if a black government works in Zimbabwe without destroying everything that's white, it might point to our salvation down here. Until then we see only Congos and Ugandas.'

They were getting close now and they became silent. Helen switched off her headlights as they neared the township, and a few moments later they saw the tail lights of Kyller's Land Rover glow more brightly as he braked to a stop. Helen slowed the sports car to a crawl, the engine barely ticking over.

The low silhouette of the first row of small bungalow houses became faintly visible in the darkness. They were only a hundred yards away from the edge of the township.

'Pull off the road and stop,' Falcon murmured softly.

Helen obeyed, turning on to a patch of wasteland and allowing the car to roll clear of the road before she switched off the engine. Ahead the Land Rover had stopped where the road entered the town.

They heard sharp voices as Kyller was challenged, but they were not close enough to see how many men formed the reception committee. Kyller had switched off his engine and his vehicle lights went out.

'Wait here,' Falcon said, and started to get out of the car.

Helen stopped him, her hand closing quickly on his arm.

'Mark, where do you think you're going?'

'To follow Kyller.'

'Into Soweto? Mark, you'd have to be crazy. Soweto is dangerous for whites. Only the police ever go in there, and they only go in force with dogs and guns and water cannon. Kyller's got a black escort, but you'd probably be killed as soon as they spotted your white face.'

Falcon hesitated, knowing that she was right. Soweto was a familiar name in world headlines, a festering sore of frustration and hate. Its dirt streets had one of the highest crime rates in the world. It was a place where mugging and violence were an everyday affair.

'Mark, they murder each other in there, so they certainly wouldn't hesitate to murder a stray white man. I'm telling you, it would be easier for an infidel to penetrate medieval Mecca, than for a white to go into black Soweto.'

'Okay,' Falcon decided. 'We'll wait and see what happens. But we're not going to wait in the car like a couple of sitting ducks.'

Helen showed a brief smile of approval, and together they got out of the car. They moved forward cautiously, covering half the distance toward Kyller's Land Rover which now stood abandoned in the empty street. Kyller and his escort had gone on foot into the huge maze of box-like, one-storey houses.

Falcon paused, the frustration growing inside him. But Soweto brooded like a sullen, living thing. He could feel its all-enveloping hostility, reflected inward and outward. It was like being on the edge of a malevolent jungle, or a poisonous swamp. To go further would be inviting disaster.

Falcon did not lack courage, but neither was he a fool. He pulled gently on Helen's hand and led her to one side, so that they were well clear of the road leading back to their parked car.

They lay flat in the long dry grass of a shallow gulley, and shrouded by darkness they waited.

Mike Kyller had been led for half a mile through the dirt streets of Soweto, and the endless rows of drab brick houses, each with its identical roof of dull brown corrugated asbestos, had all fallen silent in turn as he and his six-man escort passed. They were battery chicken huts on a monstrous scale, and the atmosphere alone was almost enough to strangle the single white man.

It was a night too hot for sleep and there were large groups of men, youths and girls, loitering in the roadway. They stared after Kyller with sullen eyes and he was equally aware of the hundreds of hidden eyes behind the windows and walls. He stayed close to his guides, especially the huge Zulu with the close-shaved dome head. Without their protection Kyller knew he would be quickly torn to pieces.

The house they finally entered was exactly the same as all the others, a three-room brick box. Six men were already squashed into the largest room, most of them drinking beer. They wore camouflage combat jackets and black berets. Their badge was a red disc with a black K.

Kyller was pushed inside, accompanied by the Zulu giant. The rest of his escort stayed back, crowding the doorway.

'He is here,' Nicholas Temela said briefly, and spat on the floor to underline his contempt for the white man.

Jonas Kitaka was seated at a bare wooden table, with the rest of his aides lounging around or behind him. He stood up and smiled a greeting, his teeth gleamed white, but somehow ugly and menacing in the thick black bush of his beard. He was a big man with a barrel chest, not quite as big as his towering second-in-command, but he managed to exude an aura of even more strength and power.

'So you came, Sergeant Mike. For a time I thought you might run away.'

There were chuckles and hoots, from the men visible and from others unseen in the other two rooms. They were happy to see the white man humiliated.

Kyller was sweating. He knew his face glistened in the harsh glare of light from the single bulb suspended from the ceiling. He said hoarsely, 'Tell me what you want, Jonas. Let's get it over.'

Kitaka's humourless smile lingered for a moment, playing cat and mouse. He knew his men would appreciate more sport, but Kyller was under heavy pressure and he did not want his former comrade-in-arms to crack. There was serious business to be concluded first.

He said bluntly, 'You know what I want, Sergeant Mike. We have a deal. Now you must keep your side of it. I need your helicopter tomorrow night.'

Kyller stared at him. 'Tomorrow—? That's impossible. It's too soon. You have to give me more time.'

'Time for what?' Kitaka's eyes were hot black coals that seemed to blaze and burn into Kyller's brain. 'Time to get drunk? Time to decide whether you have the guts to betray us to the white police? Or just time to run away and hide? You have already had a month, Sergeant Mike. Time enough to decide all these things.'

'It's not my helicopter,' Kyller protested. 'I only fly it for Jacobsen. I have to figure out how to use it without him knowing. Twenty-four hours is too short notice.'

'The first phase of operation *Firestrike* will begin in twenty-four hours,' Nicholas Temela snapped curtly. 'The timetable cannot be changed.'

Kyller twisted to face the tall Zulu. 'Firestrike? What's that? You haven't told me anything of what this is all about.'

'There is no need for you to know.' Kitaka's voice was a whiplash at Kyller, while his eyes shot a sharp warning to Temela. 'All you have to do is to bring your helicopter to a certain spot at a certain time.'

He produced a large-scale map of South Africa and unfolded it on the table, turning it so that it was the right way up for Kyller to read.

'Here is the place, east of the Blyde River Canyon, only twenty miles outside the Kruger Park. You will return to the game park tomorrow morning. One of my men will travel with you. He will show you the exact spot where you must rendezvous with the helicopter.'

Kyller moved forward to look down at the forefinger stabbing the map. He swallowed hard. 'Why, Jonas? You gotta tell me why?'

Kitaka leaned back in his chair, his lip curling into a sneer. 'Because of what happened in the Congo, Sergeant Mike. That is your only reason why. Your secret, which I have kept for so many years. Silence has its price, and mine has been a long silence. Now you can pay for it.'

Kyller stared at him. 'Is that all, Jonas?'

Kitaka nodded. 'That is all. Be there at midnight, and make sure the fuel tanks are full before you take off. We shall need your maximum range.' He saw doubt in Kyller's eyes and offered a smile and some hope. 'All these years, Sergeant Mike, I have kept your secret for nothing. Until I needed you for this I had forgotten the whole thing. When you have done this one service for me, I shall forget again.'

'Okay,' Kyller agreed. He licked his lips and found them dry.

Kitaka laughed, recognizing the need. 'Have a beer, Sergeant Mike, for old times' sake.'

He made a signal and one of his aides threw a full beer can. It hit Kyller on the chest and he fumbled to hold it. Temela took the can away, pulled off the ring tab and grinned broadly as he handed it back. More beer cans were tossed cheerfully around the room.

Kitaka made a toast. 'To the Congo.'

Kyller choked.

'Drink,' Kitaka urged ferociously.

Reluctantly Kyller drank the beer. He hoped they would take him back to the Land Rover before they got too drunk, and then he remembered that he still had another problem.

'The newspaper man — Falcon — he followed me.'

'Forget him.' Kitaka propped his feet on the table and waved a carelessly dismissive hand. 'By this time your meddlesome friend is already dead.'

On the edge of the township two groups of shadows had filtered out into the darkened wasteland. They formed a menacing pincer movement to encircle the black Lancia sports car, and when the wide circle was complete it began to tighten. The crouched men and youths straightened their backs, making taller silhouettes in the gloom. Now they could afford to abandon stealth and began to whistle, making soft hoots and cat-calls. They had no need to rush, but when one impatient youth broke into a run the others joined in the mad stampede.

Their howls of elation quickly turned into howls of cheated rage as they discovered that the car was empty. Many of them carried sticks and bicycle chains and they quickly vented their displeasure on the vehicle. The heavy blows and the smashing of glass headlights and windows echoed above the babble of shouts and curses.

Fifty yards away Falcon lay flat in the low dip beside Helen. He tapped her arm and when she turned her head he made a silent signal to withdraw. Carefully they began to wriggle backwards through the long grass.

The mob were arguing with mounting anger and excitement. Some of the younger men began to rock the car from side to side. More joined in and quickly heaved it over with a thunderous crash. Loud cheers went up. The car spilled petrol and an eager hand threw a lighted match. With a roar the car exploded in red flames.

Helen paused in their retreat and looked bitterly at Falcon. 'It's what we should have expected. And what has it proved?'

'I'm sorry about the car,' Falcon said softly. 'But it's proved we can't trust Mike Kyller. He's had the benefit of the doubt, and the next time we meet I'll feel justified in beating the truth out of him.'

'Big deal,' Helen muttered sourly. 'If he's got any sense we'll never see him again.'

'Damn,' Falcon said and gripped her arm hard to shut her up. Helen heard the new danger in the same moment and froze.

Most of the mob were still dancing around the burning car, but a few of their leaders were shouting to organize a further search. More men were running to the scene and with them ran two barking mongrel dogs.

There was no need for words and with renewed urgency Falcon and Helen continued their retreat, widening the gap between themselves and the mob as quickly as possible as they backed into the night and the low scrub. More and more people were spilling out from the township, both men and women, some of them running to join the fun at the bonfire, the others spreading out and yelling at each other as they searched the wasteland.

Abruptly the yapping of the dogs became positive and hysterical. The clamour of the mob became crystallized in pursuit.

Falcon straightened up, knowing the dogs had got their scent. 'Run!' he snapped.

Helen obeyed and they burst into flight, knowing that speed was their only hope. Behind them the howls of the mob took on a triumphant new note as the dim outlines of the fugitives were spotted in the night. The chase began in earnest to run them down.

Alone Falcon would have stayed ahead. He still had the strength and stamina that had been tested to the limit with full-pack, twenty-mile fast route marches during his service days, but beside him Helen soon began to falter and stumble. Disaster came when she tripped over a stump of bush and was flung sprawling.

Falcon heard her yelp of pain and turned to pick her up. She rose quickly with his help, but then almost fell again when she tried to put her weight on her right foot. She hung on to him for support, hopping in anguish on one leg.

'Oh, God,' she groaned. 'I've twisted my ankle.'

Falcon promptly threw her over his shoulder and continued their flight, but the forerunners of the mob were fast closing the gap. When he turned his head to check on his enemies he saw that he was hopelessly outnumbered. They came for him with furious determination and he knew they intended to kill both himself and Helen by beating them to a crude and bloody pulp.

CHAPTER 7

Falcon lowered Helen to the ground. There was still time for him to escape alone, but her face was terror-stricken and he knew he could not leave her. The victory cries of the mob shrieked through the night and he stepped forward to meet them.

The first to charge in for the kill was a slender, sinewy youth of about twenty. He carried a pick-axe handle and leaped forward with a wild war whoop and a swinging blow that would have knocked Falcon's head from his shoulders if it had landed.

But the Falcon was no easy kill. He ducked under the sweep of the heavy hardwood club. His shoulder crashed into the man's chest, cracking ribs and driving the air from the collapsing lungs. The youth fell as though he had been a victim of his own blow, and Falcon wrenched the pick-axe handle from his grasp before he hit the ground.

In the Falcon's hands the pick-axe handle became a truly devastating weapon. With a series of fast, whirling blows he smashed down the next three sprinters who reached him almost simultaneously. The next wave shouted warnings to each other and held back, waiting for the slow runners, the heavier men who formed the bulk of the mob, to catch up.

In less than a minute the two fugitives were surrounded. The irate Africans had fanned out in a loose circle to cut them off and they were trapped in the darkened wasteland. A few stars glinted through the black clouds overhead, just enough to show the ring of threatening shadows looming closer.

The mob was at least thirty strong, building up rapidly with stragglers still catching up after the long run from the township. They were too many even for the Falcon, and when their leaders urged them into a concerted rush from all sides he knew it was the end. Like jackals surging on a wounded lion they swamped him.

For an incredible three minutes he held them off, and then he went down fighting with three men on his back and two more hanging on to each arm. Fists and bare feet thudded into him from all directions and he heard Helen scream. He began to black out.

It was then he heard the roar of approaching vehicles. The voices of the mob changed from glee to panic as bright headlights stabbed through the night, and then the sharp crack of a revolver shot made them scatter.

Falcon pushed himself painfully up on to his knees and saw the three police cars bounce to a stop as they raced up over the rough terrain. The doors flew open on each vehicle and a dozen armed policemen spilled out into the dust and dirt clouds churned up by the skidding wheels. A whole volley of revolver shots punctuated the screams and shrieks of alarm to further disperse the mob. Most of the bullets were aimed into the crowd, and only a few over their heads.

'Be still, man!' A voice ordered Falcon, and he froze beside Helen.

He watched as two vicious Alsatian dogs were unleashed to chase the fleeing Africans back across the scrubland. The snarls and the screams slowly faded, and it seemed a long time before the white police officers finally blew their whistles to recall the dogs.

A fourth police car arrived a few minutes later. The officer in charge of the first three vehicles hurried to report to the large, hard-faced man who sat in the front passenger seat. The big man scowled as he listened and then got out of the car. He wore a grey suit, a contrast to the paramilitary uniforms of the riot police around him, and obviously he was in overall command.

Falcon and Helen had been helped to their feet, bruised and battered and marked with superficial cuts. They were led over to face the big man who scowled again to show his disapproval. He was in his fifties with short hair and hard balls of grey granite for eyes. His white shirt was open at the thick red neck. He looked like a sunburned Boer farmer, but his attitude was pure bull cop.

'So you are the cause of all this trouble.' His voice was harsh, the Afrikaner accent as strong as any Falcon had yet heard during his short stay in South Africa. 'What's it all about, man? Hey?'

'We were attacked,' Falcon said briefly. His ribs had taken a pummelling and he hadn't quite recovered his breath. 'They set our car on fire and chased us into the scrub.'

'I can see that, man. You think I am blind.' He flung out an impatient arm to point back toward Soweto, where the flames from the burning car still licked up against the dark skyline. 'We saw the fire. That's what brought my patrol to investigate. You were lucky, man — damned lucky!'

'I realize that.' Falcon tried a crooked smile. 'I'm sure you saved our lives. We owe you our thanks, Inspector—?'

'Colonel,' the big man corrected. 'I am Colonel Weissner. And who the hell are you?'

Falcon told him, introducing Helen at the same time. Weissner looked unimpressed by their names, and frankly disgusted by their occupation.

'Journalists, hey? You think that gives you some right to be stupid? No whites come out to this Bantu hellhole at night! No whites are allowed here at all without a police permit! You are a visitor in this country, you do not know better. But you—' He stabbed a thick finger angrily at Helen. 'You are South African. You know the law.'

Helen was pale and shaken. There was a bruise over her eye and a trickle of blood at the corner of her lower lip. She said hesitantly, 'We didn't go into Soweto. We stopped outside the township.'

'Why? You better have a damn good reason for being there.' His hostile eyes flashed back to Falcon. 'You think we don't have enough bloody nosey foreign journalists coming out here to write about how bad we treat the Bantu? Well now you've just had a taste of how the Bantu would treat us if they had half a chance. They were going to tear you to pieces, man, just because you were white.'

Helen said quickly, 'We didn't come for that kind of story.'

'What then?'

'We followed a man out here.' She faltered for a moment and then blurted it all. 'His name is Mike Kyller. He said he could lead us to Jonas Kitaka.'

Weissner stared at her, then at Falcon. Then he spoke softly for the first time.

'Kitaka? He is here? In Soweto?'

'We don't know,' Falcon told him. 'We never found out.'

Weissner turned his head slowly to gaze back over the wasteland toward the invisible sprawl of the black township.

The Lancia sports car had burned out and now there was only a pall of spreading smoke thickening the darkness.

'I think,' he said at last, 'that you must both return to Johannesburg with me. There is much explaining you have to do.'

It was the beginning of a long night. They were taken to a central police station, separated into two small bare rooms, and thoroughly interrogated by Weissner and relays of his aides. Through it all Falcon stuck to the same story he had already given Helen. He had met Kyller by chance in the Golden Crescent, casually dropped the name of Jonas Kitaka, and had been given an unexpected lead to a possible story. It was almost the whole truth, and he hoped that Helen was not telling them anything different.

Weissner frequently left the room where Falcon was held, either to take a break or to check Falcon's answers with Helen's. Although once Falcon heard the big man tell one of his colleagues that he had to make another call to Pretoria.

By morning Falcon had decided that Weissner was not just an ordinary policeman. He was in command, but there was a cold gulf between the red-necked colonel and the men who obeyed his orders. The respect they showed him was more than that due to a senior officer in the same force. It was too deferential, too guarded.

So Weissner was something higher, a power above the police, which could only mean BOSS, the South African Bureau of State Security.

The realization made Falcon wonder how long had he been under surveillance by the secret police?

The hours dragged and it was noon before Weissner concluded his enquiries. Then Falcon and Helen were permitted to meet again over a late breakfast. Helen looked tired and pale but she ate hungrily. Falcon found that he too was ravenous and they devoted most of their attention to the large plates of bacon and eggs. With a silent police officer in attendance there was no opportunity for any private conversation.

They were drinking coffee when Weissner came into the room and joined them. He pulled a third chair up to their table and sat down, and for the first time he smiled.

'A good breakfast, hey?'

Falcon nodded politely. 'It was very good, thank you.'

He was not particularly encouraged by the smile, for he had the feeling that an old grey spider might leer in much the same way at a doomed fly which had succeeded in struggling to the edge of its web. But he asked anyway: 'Are you satisfied now, Colonel? Are we free to go?'

'Perhaps.' Weissner was in no hurry to commit himself. 'But first I thought you might be interested to know what has happened to your friend Kyller.'

'He's dead!' Helen automatically feared the worst.

'Nothing so drastic.' Weissner folded his arms on the table and watched them with speculating eyes. 'Michael Kyller returned to his apartment here in Johannesburg in the early hours of this morning. At dawn he left again in his Land Rover. He was discreetly followed by one of my men. He drove back to the Kruger National Game Park, and at this moment he is flying a party of camera-happy tourists over the Crocodile River. He has returned to his job.'

'So you don't believe us,' Falcon said wearily.

'How can I know what to believe? You accuse Kyller, but he acts like an innocent man. He goes back to his normal work.'

'You could bring him here and question him,' Falcon suggested. 'He's running scared. He might crack.'

'I could pull him in,' Weissner agreed. 'But he might not crack. If he is guilty of anything he will not talk. Not to me.' He paused shrewdly. 'But you have said that he is willing to talk to you.'

'And he led me into a trap,' Falcon reminded him.

'Perhaps, but we do not know for certain that Kyller sent the mob after you.' Weissner stopped again, his eyes fixed on Falcon's and then bluntly he spelled it out. 'What I am thinking is that you might be more successful in learning the truth from Kyller than I could hope to be. You can offer him physical violence, in the form of revenge for what happened last night — or you can offer him a substantial bribe. I leave it to you to decide which is the best way to play it, but either approach will be more credible coming from you.'

'Why should I take the risk? Last night I almost got killed.'

'Because you still want your story.' Weissner smiled again. 'And I am prepared to let you follow any track which might lead me to the *Black K* organization and Jonas Kitaka.'

He added carefully, 'If you are prepared to help me — to feed back everything you can learn from Kyller — then clearly I shall be justified in ordering your immediate release.'

Falcon knew he was being invited to set himself up again as a terrorist target, but he also recognized the veiled threat. To refuse meant that he and Helen would be detained indefinitely.

He pretended to think about it, then slowly nodded his head. 'Kyller did ask me out to the park to take a trip with him. So if you think it will help, Colonel, I'll do it.'

Falcon hired a car, a three-year-old Mercedes, to make the two-hundred-mile drive through the mountains and bushveld of the North-Eastern Transvaal. The Kruger Park occupied over 7,000 square miles in a sanctuary forty miles wide which stretched for two hundred miles along the South African side of the Mozambique border. They arrived an hour before sunset, tired, dust-stained, and having travelled too fast to really enjoy the spectacular scenery they had passed on the way.

Helen had insisted upon coming with him, after first telephoning her editor and deciding that this story held as much promise as anything else she might be doing. Falcon had tried to deter her, knowing it could get dangerous again, but in the end he had given way. He had to admit that he enjoyed her company, and that her language and local background knowledge could still prove invaluable.

She had done her fair share of the driving, enabling them to make a nonstop journey, but she was asleep in the passenger seat when Falcon drove the last lap to enter the park boundary. The dirt road continued through long grass and bush country and he saw glimpses of giraffe and antelope before he found the tourist rest camp of thatch-roofed white huts and small bungalows.

He saw the parked helicopter on the far side of the camp. It was a Fairchild Hiller 1000, the fuselage painted tawny yellow with dark leopard spots. A wooden office building a few yards away bore a large sign saying LEOPARD SAFARIS.

Falcon stopped the car outside the office, and for a moment he looked thoughtfully at the helicopter. Beside him Helen woke up, yawned and stretched her stiff muscles.

A man came out to meet them. He was about thirty, suntanned, wearing bush shirt and shorts and a strip of leopard fur around his soft-brimmed hat. Falcon guessed the image was just right for the female tourists.

'Hi there,' he greeted them cheerfully. 'I'm Cornelius Jacobsen. I run this outfit.' He jerked a thumb over his shoulder where a young blonde woman had followed him out of the office. 'That's Lena. My wife. She does all the bookwork. Runs the show really. I just fly the chopper.' His grin was infectious. 'You people interested in taking a flight?'

'Later,' Falcon assured him. 'Right now we're looking for Mike Kyller.'

'He's airborne.' Jacobsen waved a hand at the sky. 'I run two choppers.'

'Mike told me. Business must be booming.'

'Not bad,' Jacobsen admitted. 'I can't go too low without scaring the game, so a Land Rover can still get you a closer look. But if you've got good binoculars and a really good telephoto lens on your camera, I can practically guarantee to show you every animal in the park.'

Lena Jacobsen had drifted closer. 'Are you friends of Mike?' she asked cautiously.

'I knew him some years ago,' Falcon admitted. 'Ran into him again in Johannesburg a couple of nights back and we had a few beers together.' He sensed that both Jacobsens were ill at ease and asked, 'Is everything all right? Did Mike get back from Jo'burg okay?'

'I told you, he's flying.' Jacobsen was curt.

'Why shouldn't everything be okay?' Lena added too quickly.

Falcon shrugged. 'No reason — except I got the feeling something was bugging Mike. He was drinking a lot harder than he used to do.'

Lena frowned. 'Something's been bugging him for the past month. He was all right before. Then he stopped talking to us. That was when he started the heavy drinking.'

'It's his business,' Jacobsen said. 'We don't interfere.'

'We employ him. He flies our helicopter. It's our business when customers start to take notice.'

'Leave it alone. I told you it's probably the girl.' He looked at Falcon and explained. 'Mike has this girl in Jo'burg. I reckon she throws him over. So Mike gets sour. Give him a few weeks — he'll find another girl.'

Falcon guessed the girl was Judy, which meant Jacobsen was wrong. For it was obvious that Judy was still hopelessly in love with Kyller. However, he merely nodded agreement.

'There's a good bar and restaurant on the camp,' Jacobsen told him. 'Everybody goes there later in the evening. You people settle in and I'll tell Mike to see you there.'

'Thanks,' Falcon said. He glanced westward where the sun was a harsh red disc on the horizon and the dusk shadows were thickening in the bush. 'Isn't it getting late to be flying tourists. The light has gone for good photography.'

Jacobsen said nothing.

Lena tightened her lips, but then let out what was worrying them.

'He isn't on a tourist flight. He took off alone. We don't know where or why. He just took up one of our helicopters and disappeared.'

CHAPTER 8

The sprawling new South African Air Force base was one of the biggest military installations in the Transvaal. It was a vast complex of runways, hangars, control buildings, store buildings, fuel dumps and barrack blocks. Rows of sleek Mirage strike fighter jets stood poised facing north, ready to combat any violation of South African air space by Cuban or black-piloted MiGs. Beside them were smaller numbers of the French-built Alouette helicopters used to patrol the hostile borders with Zimbabwe and Mozambique.

South African Army units guarded the base. Dog handlers roamed the open spaces between the runways, and the entire area was surrounded by a ten-foot-high steel-mesh fence topped with barbed wire.

The base was a hard nut to crack, but it was also the target for the first phase of the operation codenamed *Firestrike*.

It was after sunset when a ten-ton army truck approached the main gates. The army had been engaged on manoeuvres throughout the day and the big trucks had been passing in and out, loaded with troops, with unusual frequency. This one was late returning, but on this particular day it was no cause for suspicion.

The truck carried a dozen well-armed black Africans in the uniforms of regular soldiers. But the Bantu formed twenty per cent of the lower ranks of the South African armed forces, so this again was no immediate cause for suspicion.

No one had counted the number of trucks going out, and the barrier was raised and the truck was casually waved through.

Behind the steering wheel of the ten-tonner Jonas Kitaka smiled happily and gave a sloppy, semi-military salute in return.

He drove the truck away from the gates, deeper into the base complex, and heading in the general direction of the army barrack blocks and parade ground where the soldiers would normally disembark. He waited until he was out of sight of the military policemen at the gates before he turned sharp right and accelerated past the service hangars and the runways toward the western perimeter fence.

On the eastern side of the air base were the motor pools and fuel dumps. They were only fifty yards from the fence and it was here that Nicholas Temela led a slightly larger force of guerrillas in a sabotage attack that was spectacular in effect but intended purely as a diversion. The big Zulu had twenty men under his command, all of them blatantly wearing their *Black K* insignia.

Under cover of darkness they wriggled close to the fence. Temela and three others carried wire cutters and it was only a few minutes work to cut their way through. Temela left four men to stand guard over their line of retreat, with orders to deal with any patrolling sentries who might come by, and led the others forward in a stealthy belly crawl up to the fuel dumps.

They had brought with them four of the Russian-made limpet mines which they had used with such dramatic effect on power stations and oil refineries elsewhere, and attached them to four fully-loaded fuel trucks parked beside the biggest underground dump. Temela set the timing devices for a bare three minutes, for this was a rare occasion when they did not intend to be halfway back to Mozambique when the big bang went up.

They backed off and Temela split his remaining men into two eight-man squads. He led one group off to the left to take up prone firing positions between the fuel dumps and the nearest guard huts. The second group moved right, crawling toward the nearest Mirage parked on the runway.

Kitaka slowed the truck as he approached the inner guard barrier protecting the high security zone on the western side of the huge air base. Two white South African military policemen levelled their submachine guns and one of them barked a sharp command to halt.

Kitaka braked the truck to a stop, put the gear in neutral and pulled on the handbrake. He leaned his head and shoulders out of the open window and asked cheerfully,

'Hey, man, where's the troop barracks for the new soldiers?'

The guard moved up to him warily. 'How come you don't know?'

'We're a new intake, man. We only just arrived. Just finished basic training.'

'Sergeant.' The guard touched his stripes. 'You call me Sergeant. Don't they teach you dumb Bantu anything in training camp?'

'No, sir. I mean yes, sir — Sergeant, sir.' Kitaka made an apologetic shrug. 'Which way is our barracks, Sergeant, sir?'

'You took a wrong turn after you came through the main gates,' the sergeant told him. 'You turned right when you should have turned left.'

He lowered his submachine gun and pointed back the way the truck had come. His shoulder was touching the cab door as he began to give them careful directions, repeating every move twice as though he was explaining to a very dull child.

The second man of the guard detail had moved up to the opposite side of the truck. He glanced into the cab, staring for a moment at the impassive face of the silent African who sat beside Kitaka with his hands folded innocently in his lap. Then without speaking the white policeman moved away, strolling toward the back of the truck to check inside.

The two white men were now separated on opposite sides of the truck. The African in the front passenger seat reached over and touched Kitaka's knee, the signal that the moment was right.

Kitaka reached down through the window and cupped a big hand under the guard sergeant's chin, hauling the man back and up onto his toes. It was an effective way of shutting the man's mouth and exposing his throat at the same time. Before the startled man could even begin to struggle Kitaka had brought out the razor-sharp commando knife in his right hand and made one vicious slicing movement. The force of the blow severed the sergeant's windpipe and most of his neck.

Kitaka's companion had slipped out of the cab on the opposite side. In two fast, padding strides he had caught up with the second guard and a black hand was clamped hard over the white mouth before it could open to raise the alarm. This time the knife blade was slammed up beneath the ribs from behind, spearing the heart.

Kitaka was out of the cab and around the front of the truck in time to see the second guard fall. He grinned, and rapped lightly twice on the side of the truck with the hilt of his bloodied knife. The lashings securing the canvas hood at the back were slashed open and the rest of his assault force leaped out. They had AK-47 combat rifles slung across their shoulders, but knives ready in hand for more silent killing.

They followed Kitaka as he ducked under the pole barrier and fanned out to silently encircle the guard hut further inside the compound. The windows were open and they deftly tossed inside what looked like ordinary smoke bombs. There was a slight clatter as the cannisters rolled across the floor inside the building, but no explosion. Instead of smoke the cannisters immediately began to exude thick clouds of poisonous gas.

There were six soldiers on duty call inside the guard hut, and only two of them succeeded in clawing their way out into the open air. They were dying on their feet, vomiting and choking helplessly, and the sharp knives finished them off.

Black K had captured the high-security compound and so far not a shot had been fired.

Thirty seconds later, on the far side of the camp, the four fuel trucks exploded. Two of them went up simultaneously and the other two followed seconds later in swift succession. The sleeping air base was shocked awake by the rolling thunders of sound, and the brilliant scarlet and orange fireballs lit up the fuel dumps and motor pools as brightly as though it were daylight.

The men in the nearest guard huts grabbed for their pants and weapons and ran to the scene, only to be cut down by bursts of murderous automatic rifle fire as Nicholas Temela and his guerrillas sprang their ambush.

The men of the second squad which Temela had detached to stalk the runways now rushed the final few yards and hurled hand grenades at the nearest Mirage fighter. The aircraft blew up into another raging inferno.

The base became a disturbed hornet's nest of feverish activity. Telephones jangled and the lines were jammed and confused as senior officers shouted orders and demanded information. A red alert sounded and troops were rushed toward the flaming holocaust that now belched huge black smoke clouds to the sky.

Temela and his men began to break away, retreating toward their entry holes in the fence, but fighting a deliberately noisy rearguard action to keep the defending forces occupied.

Kitaka had donned a gas mask and dived into the death-filled guard hut. He found the body of the lieutenant in charge of the guard detail and quickly robbed the dead man of his keys. He emerged again and threw the gas mask away as he led his men in a silent run to the sloping concrete ramp which led down to the locked doors of the main underground bomb store.

Kitaka unlocked the heavy steel doors and they passed inside. They continued at a run down the brightly lit, sloping concrete tunnel, and within seconds they were inside the storeroom. All around them were steel racks bristling with air-to-air and air-to-surface rocket missiles ready to arm the Mirage jets. Kitaka ignored them, and also the stacked boxes of canon shells. What he wanted was at the far end of the underground chamber, supported by a specially constructed treble sling cradle. They looked like three huge artillery shells, each one six feet long with four short guidance fins at the base. Their polished steel casings had an evil gleam under the harsh strip lighting set in the low ceiling.

Kitaka knew he had no time to waste. He spotted a rubber wheeled loading trolley and yelled orders. His companions grabbed the trolley and manhandled one of the huge shells on to it. They started to strap it in place for safer handling but Kitaka yelled at them to get moving. A few of the terrorists rolled fearful eyes, they were already sweating profusely, but they obeyed and pushed the trolley at a run, back through the underground chamber and up the ramp.

The ten-ton truck had been backed up to the top of the ramp. The tailboard was down and their prize was hauled on board. A pile of blankets made a soft bed, and ropes had been provided to hold it secure. The raiding party scrambled on board and Kitaka swung back behind the wheel. He started the engine and immediately drove off.

He was not fool enough to attempt to drive back through the main gates. That sort of bluff could only work once. Instead he turned the truck onto one of the runways, drove hard for a hundred yards, and then swerved onto the rough grass to drive directly for the perimeter fence.

A two-man foot patrol came running to intercept them, but a burst from an AK-47 cut the two men down. They were the first shots Kitaka's party had fired, and he hoped they would pass unnoticed against the background of the fierce battle still raging on the far side of the camp.

He stopped the truck against the fence and two of his men sprang out with heavy bolt croppers to attack the steel mesh. Quickly they cut a gateway and the truck passed through.

Kitaka drove on over the rough terrain, using no headlights and swerving frequently as bush and trees loomed up out of the darkness, and taking a calculated risk with the violent, jolting movement.

He was sweating almost as much as his men when at last the truck lurched onto a paved road. He turned south, switched on his lights, and drove at full speed for his rendezvous.

On the east side of the air base Temela had left three of his men dead, but the rest had withdrawn through the fence. They were still shooting into the camp, where the fires had spread and more vehicles and fuel drums were exploding to add to the panic and confusion.

Not until they had exhausted the last magazine of ammunition did the big Zulu give the order to scatter and melt away into the bush.

Mike Kyller was waiting with the helicopter on a patch of level grassland, screened by a large clump of mopani bush from the road where it forked back north toward the Blyde River Canyon. He had noticed the faint red glow of the flames lighting up the distant skyline to the north-east, and there was a thick swirling of fear in his belly.

He was hating himself for double-crossing Cornelius Jacobsen, who had proved a good friend as well as a fair employer. But most of all he found himself hating Jonas Kitaka for forcing him faster and deeper into something which was obviously far bigger and more dangerous than he had ever thought possible.

When the army truck roared up out of the night he felt a surge of panic. He backed away from the helicopter, taking cover in the bush as the truck stopped. He recognized the South African army uniforms of the men who leaped out of the truck and hurried toward the helicopter through the gloom, and his heart seemed to rise on the fear tide and jam in his throat.

'Sergeant Mike!'

Kitaka paused beneath the rotor blade and peered left and right as he called Kyller's name. Slowly the ex-mercenary came out into the open. There was a look of horror on his face as he stared at the stolen uniforms, but the shock deepened when he saw the large steel shell-shape they unloaded from the truck and carried hastily toward the waiting helicopter.

Kyller recognized it as a missile of some kind, but it was too fat and heavy to be an ordinary air-to-air or air-to-surface rocket. One of those would have been more streamlined, more slender. This thing was something infinitely more terrible.

Kyller came near to fainting when one of the loading party stumbled and they almost dropped it.

'Jonas,' he choked hoarsely. 'For God's sake, man — what have you done?'

'Shut your mouth,' Kitaka snapped. He yanked open the door of the helicopter and scrambled inside. The FH-1000 was a five-seater and he helped to haul in the gleaming silver weapon and lay it across the rear seats.

'I'm not flying that,' Kyller protested. 'You hear me, Jonas. I want out.'

Kitaka jumped back to earth. The big commando knife was in his hand and he used the point to lift Kyller's chin. There was blood still wet on the blade.

'Now you hear me, Sergeant Mike. You get in that pilot seat and fly. There's no way now you can back out.'

Kyller sweated but stood his ground. 'What's the difference, Jonas? You can kill me now — or I'll hang later.'

'I won't kill you, Sergeant Mike. I'll just talk a little.' Kitaka's smile was cruel and confident. 'Remember the Congo, Sergeant Mike? Remember that little town we liberated from the Simbas? Remember that bungalow we searched for loot?'

Kyller remembered. His face sickened with anguish. The memory was a burden of guilt and disgust with himself that he had carried for too many years.

Kitaka went on brutally, 'You remember the white woman we found tied naked to the bed. You needed a lot of whisky courage that day before we went into action, and you had more after. And when you saw that white pussy all ready and waiting, you couldn't resist it. You raped her, Sergeant Mike. Not the Simbas. Man, you were lucky she had that heart attack and died.'

Kyller groaned and squeezed his eyes shut.

Kitaka put the knife away and slapped him on the shoulder.

'But I covered up for you, Sergeant Mike. I told our dumb white officers that the woman must have been raped by Simbas and that she was dead when we found her. They believed it. They can go on believing it. There's still no need for the other whites in Nine Commando to ever know.'

Kyller was beaten and he knew it. He let Kitaka steer him over to the helicopter and climbed up into his seat.

Kitaka climbed up beside him. There was only room now for the two of them and the terrorist leader shouted orders to send his followers running back to the truck.

'They'll drive north up the canyon road,' he told Kyller. 'They'll dump the truck and the uniforms and split. With some luck the security forces will think we're heading north too, they'll expect us to try for the nearest border. So we go south. Take her up, Sergeant Mike. Let's move it!'

Kyller had no choice. He started the rotors and whirled the helicopter aloft, heading due south as he had been ordered.

CHAPTER 9

Jacobsen was uncomfortable and reluctant to talk. He was a man who believed in minding his own business, and gave other men the same respect for privacy he expected to receive. It took Falcon a full five minutes of tactful persuasion before he would elaborate on what his wife had already told them.

It was not much. Kyller had returned to the park shortly before noon, looking tired and strained. He had rested for an hour, and then made two separate one-hour tourist flights during the course of the afternoon. Jacobsen had also been busy throughout the day, and the two men had not spent any time on the ground together. After his last scheduled flight Kyller had refuelled his helicopter, supposedly ready for the next day. Ten minutes before Jacobsen was due back Kyller had unexpectedly taken off again and flown due west.

'I tried to call him up on the radio,' Lena Jacobsen said. 'But he wouldn't answer. Cornelius tried when he got back with Lima One, but Mike wouldn't talk to him either.'

'His radio could be out,' Jacobsen defended Kyller. 'We've had Lima Two for six years. She was second-hand when we bought her.'

'There was nothing wrong with his radio,' Lena insisted tartly.

Falcon realized they had been arguing about it before he and Helen had arrived. Lena, the efficient businesswoman, clearly did not think too highly of Mike Kyller, while her husband was showing the stubborn loyalty of male camaraderie.

Before they could get too heated he asked quietly: 'Have you any idea where he might have been going?'

Jacobsen shrugged helplessly. Lena pursed her lips and shook her head.

'So in effect, he's stolen your helicopter.'

'Borrowed it,' Jacobsen said. 'He'll bring it back. Mike knew I wouldn't say no if he wanted to use it.'

'But he didn't ask.' The sun had set and the short dusk had deepened into darkness, and he added pointedly: 'And it doesn't look as though he intends to bring it back tonight.'

Jacobsen frowned and said nothing.

Helen spoke for the first time. 'What sort of helicopter is Mike flying?'

'Another FH-1000,' Lena answered. 'We have two of the same model. The only difference is that we bought Lima One two years ago, brand new. That's when we hired Kyller to pilot Lima Two.'

Falcon looked again at the outline of the parked helicopter. He knew the model. It was one used mainly for civilian use, but it had grown initially out of a US Army specification for a high speed light observation helicopter. The two-bladed semi-rigid teetering rotor had an automatic stabilizing system, and the turbine engine and power controls had been in advance of anything else in the civilian field when it had first appeared. With seats for four passengers and the pilot it had a maximum speed of 127mph, with a range of almost three hundred and fifty miles.

It was a useful and versatile machine, ideal for Jacobsen's purpose. No doubt it was ideal for Kyller's purpose too, whatever it might be.

He looked back to Jacobsen. The pilot's face was stubborn in the gloom and Falcon knew he had to play upon the man's loyalty to win his cooperation.

'Mister Jacobsen,' he said carefully. 'I know Mike is a friend of yours, and you don't want to talk about him behind his back. I appreciate that. But Mike is a friend of mine too, and I think he's got himself into some big trouble. More than he can handle. And if we're going to help him we have to find out what he's doing.'

'What sort of trouble?' Jacobsen was suspicious.

'I don't know. Mike started to tell me in Jo'burg. Then he clammed up. But something's eating him inside. Something made him hit the bottle. He needs our help.'

'Okay,' Jacobsen said. 'I'll try again to raise him on the radio.'

'He won't answer.' Lena was certain. 'You've already tried a hundred times.'

'What then, for Christ's sake?'

Falcon had recognized Kyller's battered yellow Land Rover which was parked beside one of the thatched rondavel huts. He pointed toward it and made a suggestion.

'I guess that's where he sleeps when he's on camp. We could take a look inside. There may be something to give us a lead.'

'No, man.' The stiffness was back in Jacobsen's voice. 'It wouldn't be right.'

'He's your friend,' Falcon reminded him. 'And he's disappeared with one of your helicopters. That must give you some rights.'

'If he doesn't come back,' Helen said quietly, 'then eventually you will have to call in the police. They'll search his hut. It's the first thing they'll do.'

'Are you from the police?'

'No. Mark has told you, we're just friends. What I'm saying is that it must be better for his friends to go through his things now, while there's still time to help him. Rather than leave them for the police to go through later.'

'She's right,' Lena Jacobsen decided. 'Let's do it.'

She led the way over to the rondavel. Her husband still looked doubtful, but slowly he followed. Falcon smiled his thanks at Helen and they followed in turn.

Falcon paused to quickly check out the Land Rover. There was nothing which offered any possibilities except the road maps and those he brought into the rondavel. The huts were linked to an electricity supply from a generator and Jacobsen had switched on the lights.

The maps were a dead end. Nothing had been marked on them. Falcon showed them to Jacobsen and then dropped them on the bed.

The rondavel had two bedrooms, but only one of them had been used. There was a wardrobe which Lena opened to reveal a row of shirts and a couple of bush jackets on hangers. The only other piece of furniture was a dressing table, and again Falcon allowed Lena to pull open the drawers and turn over the contents. There were no clues of any kind.

Jacobsen watched his wife with definite disapproval, but did not interfere. Lena closed the last drawer and bit her lip in frustration.

'There's this!' Helen lifted a large, zip-up leather holdall bag onto the bed. It was full, but not too heavy, and it was locked.

Falcon took a penknife from his pocket, opened the blade, and began to force open the single clasp.

'Hey,' Jacobsen protested.

'It's done,' Falcon said apologetically, and ran the zip open.

It was Kyller's weekend bag, still stuffed with worn clothes and the towels and shaving kit he had used in Johannesburg. But on top was a sealed envelope, addressed in scrawled handwriting to *Cornelius Jacobsen*.

Falcon passed the letter over. 'It's to you. I think you'd better open it.'

'If Mike wanted me to read it he would have given it to me — not left it locked up in his bag.'

'I'd guess you were meant to find it. Not this soon, but later. Which means Mike must know there's a good chance he won't be coming back.' He offered the letter again. 'If you want to help him, you have to read it now.'

Jacobsen took the letter, slit open the envelope, and frowned as he studied the two handwritten pages inside. At last he handed them back to Falcon.

'Hell, man, what does it all mean?'

Falcon read swiftly, with Helen reading over his shoulder. Kyller's hand had been unsteady, probably due to the influence of drink, but the words were legible. It was the depressed and broken pattern of the man's thoughts that made the whole thing vague.

'He's making you an apology,' Falcon told Jacobsen. 'He's sorry he had to take your helicopter. But he says he is being blackmailed by something that happened in his past — he doesn't give any details. He hopes that eventually you'll get the helicopter back undamaged.'

'I got that much,' Jacobsen said impatiently. 'But the rest of it, man? That stuff about him killing somebody — or somebody killing him.'

'There's a man who is using Mike, blackmailing him.' Falcon knew the reference had to mean Jonas Kitaka, but at this stage he saw no reason to add to what Jacobsen had already read. 'Mike thinks this man is going to kill him when the job is over. It doesn't say what the job is, but afterwards Mike will know too much. Mike has figured it out, and he intends to try and kill this other man, the blackmailer, first. If he succeeds he was going to come back and destroy this letter. If he fails, you'll find it and know what's happened.'

Falcon looked up. 'That's pretty much what we expected.'

'There was something about the girl?'

Falcon nodded. 'Judy Luys. There's a Johannesburg address. She's in the apartment next door to Mike's. He's got a bank account, and he says here some wages due. He wants all that, and anything you can get from selling the Land Rover to go to the girl. He knows he's been a bastard to her. He wants to make it up.'

'Poor bloody Mike,' Jacobsen said. 'What the hell has he got himself into?'

'He doesn't say, but there's something here in this last paragraph which could help us to find out. He's flying your helicopter to a rendezvous six miles due east of the north end of the Blyde River Canyon. Where's that?'

'It's a scenic area, nature reserve — about forty miles west of here.'

Lena reached for the letter. Falcon let her take it. He kept his eyes fixed on Jacobsen.

'How do you feel about night flying?'

'Man, you're on!' The doubts had all been swept away, the stubborn loyalty transformed into a hard new determination.

'Good,' Falcon smiled. 'I'm hiring your helicopter.'

'No need, man. This is no tourist flight. This one's free for Mike.' He turned to his wife. 'Lena, you stay with the radio. Call us up if Mike comes back with Lima Two.'

'Sure.' Lena nodded. 'In the meantime I'll call the police.'

'No.' Jacobsen ordered sharply. 'We'll find Mike first. Give him a chance. Maybe we can sort it out.'

Lena shrugged, but decided not to argue.

Falcon and Jacobsen hurried to climb on board the helicopter, and as they strapped themselves in there was a breathless scrambling behind them.

'You're not going without me,' Helen told them firmly.

Jacobsen glanced sideways, but Falcon made no objection. The pilot flipped the starter switches and the rotor blades began to revolve. Slowly the machine lifted upward, and then sped westward between the bright glitter of the stars and the undulating darkness of the forest and bush.

There had been no mention of time in Kyller's letter, and Falcon could only hope they were not too late.

CHAPTER 10

They saw the dull red glow on the northern skyline when they were still three miles short of the rendezvous. It was flattened by what looked like a huge bank of black cloud blotting out the stars above the horizon. The cloud bank, Falcon realized, had to be a thick pall of spreading smoke, and from the height and size he guessed that there were big oil fires burning.

'What's over there?' he asked quietly.

'Jesus Christ, man—' Jacobsen was awestruck. 'That's Hoedspruit!'

'Our frontline air base,' Helen explained grimly.

'You think they've been attacked?' Jacobsen was guessing blind. 'They've got MiGs in Mozambique now. Those bloody Russians are pouring MiGs into all the black border states.'

'They wouldn't get through.' Helen was certain. 'Our pilots would be up to intercept the second they crossed the border. Besides, most of the MiGs the Russians are giving away are out-of-date junk models. They wouldn't risk tangling with a squadron of Mirage fighters.'

'It was probably a ground attack,' Falcon agreed with her. 'Another hit-and-run sabotage job.'

'By *Black K*?'

The name caused Jacobsen to twist round in his seat and stare at Helen's face, momentarily forgetting both his controls and the burning skyline.

'Hey, what is this? What the hell has Mike Kyller and my chopper got to do with those killers?'

'We don't know yet,' Falcon said truthfully.

'Man, you know a damn sight more than you're telling me.'

Jacobsen had shifted his challenging stare. Falcon gazed back at him calmly.

'We're only making guesses. That blaze over there, and Kyller taking off with your helicopter, are in some way connected. I don't know how — but I don't believe in coincidence either.'

'Jeeesus!' The one word was a long drawn-out expression of bewilderment and apprehension. Jacobsen's gaze flickered briefly in an automatic check over his control panel, and then shifted to fix upon the flickering glow in the distance.

'The important thing is to find that rendezvous,' Falcon reminded him. 'We're still looking for Kyller and the helicopter.'

Reluctantly Jacobsen tore his eyes away from the skyline, and resumed his concentration upon his instruments and the dark earth beneath them.

They had followed the road out of the game park, letting it lead them in a direct line due west. Now the clustered white lights of a small town showed ahead. Falcon remembered its name from the drive up in the car. Acornhoek. It straddled the T-junction where the main roads ran north and south. Jacobsen turned the helicopter to cut the corner, bypassing the town, and after a few minutes sighting the road again where it led north.

'The road forks just up here,' Jacobsen said. 'The left-hand fork goes up to Blyde River. I figure it must be close to the spot Mike was trying to describe.'

Falcon nodded. He was watching the ground now, even though the brightening red glow was directly ahead.

They saw the fork in the road approaching fast. Jacobsen slowed the helicopter and banked to the right to begin a wide circle of the area. They were all silent, searching the rugged rock and bush-tangled terrain below for a sign of Lima Two.

The level patch of ground behind the thick stands of mopani bush was the only obvious place for a helicopter to land. It was empty, but Jacobsen went low for a closer look. He switched on his spotlight and the white beam lanced down. Falcon was looking further afield and he saw a travelling blur of movement on the north-west fork of the road where it climbed up to the canyon. He pointed it out to Jacobsen and the helicopter swung in pursuit. They quickly overhauled the ten-ton army truck which was speeding without lights.

'What now?' Jacobsen demanded as he cut back his speed again to hover immediately over the truck.

Falcon was uncertain. The blacked-out truck was cause for suspicion, but it was not the missing helicopter. Again he scanned the shadowed earth and sky. His brain was racing. It took two to make a rendezvous, two people or two vehicles. Kyller and Kitaka. Lima Two and the truck. But were they ahead or too late for the rendezvous? And where was the helicopter?

'Hey!' Jacobsen shouted, and Falcon looked down.

The truck driver had panicked or lost control, and the big truck had skidded off the road to crash into the bush. Two men jumped down from the cab and more spilled out from under the canvas hood at the back. They all wore regular army combat uniforms. They scattered in all directions to run for cover, but one man turned and fired a rifle upward. The helicopter lurched up and sideways as Jacobsen soared out of range.

'Bloody hell—' the pilot said thickly. Then Helen spoke sharply to cut him short.

'There, Mark. Behind us to the left.'

Falcon twisted in his seat, looking back over his shoulder, and briefly glimpsed what she had seen as the helicopter made its sudden, evasive movement.

Behind them to the south-west were high cliffs and mountains, the beginning of the Drakensberg range which formed the spine of South Africa. Starlight glinted through a gap in the hills, and something small and distant had briefly blotted out a star which almost immediately appeared again.

It could have been a vulture or an eagle, a shred of cloud, or a trick of the starlight itself. But Falcon didn't think so. The fleeing Africans below were small fry, and all his uncertainty had vanished.

'Turn around,' he told Jacobsen. 'Head south at full speed. That's what Kyller's doing, and he's got a good start.'

Jacobsen swung the helicopter round in a tight full circle and the rotors whirled more forcefully as he gave them full power. They raced toward the dark peaks of the mountains, but now there was nothing to follow.

'Where?' Jacobsen yelled. 'Hell, man, I don't see him.'

'He's flying without lights.' Falcon was positive. 'And he's staying close under the shadow of the mountains. That's how he hopes to escape.'

They flew in tight-lipped silence for five minutes, seeing nothing ahead but the unfolding line of black mountains which now loomed close and threatening on their right flank. Jacobsen began to shoot questioning glances at Falcon, and Falcon began to doubt his own conviction.

Then they saw it again, half a mile ahead, a diminutive black dragonfly shape, glinting in the starlight where it passed another silver gap between the peaks.

'He must be crazy,' Jacobsen said. 'Hugging those mountains that tight, with no lights — he's just asking for trouble!'

'He's already in big trouble,' Falcon reminded him. 'This way he's trying to sneak out of it. How far south do these mountains go?'

'All the way south to Lesotho, and then into Cape Province,' Helen told him from behind. 'At least six hundred miles. They form the edge of the escarpment which separates the highveld from the low country along the coast.'

'So they'll give him full cover well beyond his maximum range.'

'With full tanks that's three hundred and forty-eight miles,' Jacobsen put in. 'We've clocked up sixty-five since leaving the game park. That gives him another two hundred and eighty.'

'Which puts him well south of that air base,' Falcon mused thoughtfully. 'Even if they realize a helicopter was used they will probably expect him to run north or east to the nearest border, so this way he makes a clean getaway.' He looked squarely at Jacobsen. 'I think it's time you used the radio to alert your police and air force.'

'No,' the pilot snapped harshly. 'We catch Mike first. Give him a chance, man. Maybe we can help him put things right.'

'Can we overhaul him?'

Jacobsen shrugged. 'These choppers are the same model, same weight, range, speed. But Lima Two is four years older, that means four years extra wear on the engine. So Lima One has the edge. It depends on the passenger weight Mike is carrying, but even if we can't catch up, we'll still be right behind him when he has to come down.'

Falcon knew they should use the radio now, but he couldn't afford a fight with Jacobsen. He was still dependent upon the South African's help. So he waited.

Kyller had spotted the pursuing helicopter within minutes of beginning their escape flight south. Jacobsen was flying with all his lights blazing, and Kyller only had to look over his shoulder to get the sharp taste of fear and shock. He yelled a cursing warning to Kitaka, and the terrorist leader jerked round in his seat as though he had been jabbed with an electric needle.

For several minutes Kitaka went to pieces, raving obscenities in a torrent of frustrated rage. Then he calmed down as he realized there was only one set of lights following their flight path. It was not necessarily the end, providing he could keep his cool. All he had to do was to get rid of that one trailing chopper. And do it fast. He struggled to think how.

'Slow down,' he finally ordered Kyller. 'Not too much. Just enough to let them catch up on us.'

'Why?' Kyller demanded. 'What are you gonna do?'

'You just do as you're told,' Kitaka snarled at him. 'That's all!'

The tone might have brought a dog to heel. Kyller felt a surge of anger and almost rebelled, but then he swallowed his rage and his pride. He had been a hard man once, but the years and the jungle wars had knocked most of it out of him. He didn't have the staying power, and he had never had the total ruthlessness of the power-crazed man sitting beside him.

He shut down the throttle slightly, allowing the helicopter behind to slowly pull up and close the gap.

Kitaka grinned wolfishly through his beard. The white man was soft, but he didn't want Kyller to chicken out altogether. So he waited until the gap was almost closed, and the following helicopter was less than a hundred yards from their tail before he picked up his AK-47 and slid back the cockpit window beside him.

'Now!' he barked at Kyller. 'Turn around and go back.'

Kyller began the manoeuvre, then protested as he glanced sideways and saw the muzzle of the combat rifle being pushed through the open window.

'Jonas, what the hell—'

'Do it!' Kitaka screamed at him.

Kyller froze at the controls, but the helicopter was already turning. For a moment Lima Two hung broadside across the fast-approaching nose of Lima One, and Kitaka had a clear field of fire. He emptied the full magazine and had the satisfaction of seeing the oncoming helicopter suddenly veer sideways and then plummet earthward.

He knew he had hit the pilot and let out a tribal war cry of delight. 'Okay,' he told Kyller. 'Now you can fly south again. We still got a long way to go.'

Falcon had realized what was happening as Kyller began to turn. He yelled a warning and ducked low in his seat as the red muzzle flashes appeared from the blacked-out window of Lima Two. Beside him Jacobsen was too slow or too astonished to react. The South African pilot was slammed back in his seat as the burst of bullets shattered the window in front of him and ripped into the upper part of his chest. Jacobsen was killed instantly and slumped sideways as his blood spilled, and Lima One began its death dive.

Falcon straightened up and grabbed for the controls. They were headed straight for a hard rock shoulder of mountain and there was no time to look for Kyller's machine. Jacobsen's body was in his way, the knees pushed up against the control column, but then Falcon was aware of Helen working white-faced to help him. She heaved the dead man back between the seats, giving Falcon room to take over.

He banked the helicopter with only seconds to spare, bringing it up and away from the rock face. If there had been grass growing there the rotor blades would have shaved it to a crew cut, but the rock was bare. There was a bump and a crash as the heel of one of their landing skids hit and snapped off, and then they were over the ridge. Falcon swung Lima One away from the mountain, levelled out and breathed again. His chest felt as though it was ready to burst.

He felt Jacobsen's heels bumping against his thigh as Helen gave the body a final pull, and he glanced back to see her face was white with shock. She was panting heavily from her exertions and Jacobsen's blood was on her hands. But she looked unhurt.

'He's dead,' she said in a strangled voice.

'I know,' Falcon said grimly. 'Are you okay?'

'I think so. I got down behind the seats.' She stared at him doubtfully. 'Mark, can you fly this thing?'

'I have a private pilot's licence,' he assured her. 'Don't worry about it.'

'I am worried.' She realized that he was again heading due south, still following Kyller's escape route. 'Mark, you're in the target seat now!'

'But I know what to expect.' The calm assurance was still in his voice. 'They can't pull the same trick twice now I'm watching for it.'

She was silent for a moment and then she climbed into the front passenger seat beside him. Jacobsen could no longer object, and although her hands trembled as she put on the radio headphones her voice was steady as she began to call for help.

Falcon knew it was too late for any air force helicopters from Hoedspruit to catch them up, but he didn't interfere.

Instead he concentrated on the task of giving chase and attempting to overhaul the fleeing Lima Two for the second time.

There were splashes of Jacobsen's blood on the controls and the night air streamed through the broken windshield. It was cold and fierce in his face, but he set his teeth grimly and continued to fly the straining Lima One at her maximum speed.

CHAPTER 11

It was a long chase. Kyller had not stopped to watch them go down, but had immediately continued his flight. Lima Two had pulled far ahead and thirty minutes passed before Falcon sighted her again. Kyller was still flying blind, and still keeping close to the thick black shadows thrown by the long chain of the Drakensberg.

Falcon was doing the same. Jacobsen had made the fatal mistake of flying by the regulations, with all his navigation lights brightly advertising his presence. Falcon's first move, after regaining control of the machine, had been to flip every light switch off, including the interior cabin lights. Now he was gambling on getting up close behind Lima Two before its occupants could become aware that he was still glued to their trail.

He had given Helen a couple of minutes to broadcast her message and then ordered radio silence in case Kyller should be listening for any further reports. He was hoping Kyller would assume they had crash-landed and believe the pursuit was over.

The gap closed with painful slowness. Lima One was the slightly faster machine, but only by a fraction of a mile per hour, and it took time for the gain to become noticeable. The miles blurred past in total darkness beneath them, but gradually the leading helicopter was taking shape and growing larger in the faint glimmer of starlight ahead.

Falcon was alert for any sudden narrowing of the gap, which would be the first sign of a repeat attempt of the move which had killed Jacobsen, but nothing happened. Inch by inch Lima

One pulled up behind Lima Two. Falcon hardly dared to blink and his eyes ached from the strain. Beside him Helen sat tense and equally watchful.

They were three hundred yards behind. The miles flashed by in the unfolding rock walls and rugged ranges of the escarpment to their right, and the minutes crawled.

Two hundred yards, and another eerie eternity of night miles and time slid by.

One hundred yards, and now the black dragonfly silhouette of Lima Two was sharp and clear before them, and the camouflage pattern of leopard spots was at last distinguishable in the cold starlight.

Two hundred feet, and then narrowing to one hundred feet. And Helen began to look uncertainly at Falcon. She didn't know what he intended to do, and now he was concentrating so intently that she did not dare to ask the question.

Eighty feet — and Falcon was directly behind and above the leading FH-1000 with an extra fifty feet of altitude. He was in Kyller's blind spot and staying there, and still narrowing the gap.

Fifty feet behind and thirty feet above, and suddenly the game was up. Kyller, or one of his passengers had spotted them, and suddenly Lima Two made a fast, left-hand loop.

But Falcon was ready for it. He banked Lima One to cut the corner and stayed in position above and behind the jinking machine that was struggling desperately to escape.

It was the beginning of a hair-raising duel of nerves and split-second timing, fought out in whirls, dives and loops within inches of the jagged spines of the Drakensberg. Every move that Kyller made, Falcon instantly copied, his lightning-fast reactions keeping Lima One always above and behind. Always in that safe blind spot. And always forcing Lima Two lower and lower toward the earth.

Only a matter of feet, and sometimes inches, separated the whirling disc of Kyller's rotor blades from the threatening landing skids of Falcon's undercarriage. If they touched both the skids then the rotors would shear off and shatter. Falcon would be faced with a dangerous belly-flop landing, but for Kyller it would be an instantaneous disaster. His machine would crash like a falling stone.

Falcon was giving him only one other choice, which was to go down and land.

Kyller was pouring sweat and almost choking on his own terror. He had tried every trick he knew and still he couldn't shake off the pursuing helicopter. It was sticking to him like a greyhound on a hare and it was obvious that the other pilot was trying to force him down.

From the corner of his eye he caught the glint of polished steel from the dreadful thing that lay across the rear seats and his panic almost overwhelmed him. The other pilot didn't know — couldn't possibly know — what they were carrying. If he did he would never take such suicidal and potentially catastrophic risks.

The roar of the other engine was close and he glanced up again. Through the blur of his rotors he could see the other machine nudging down again. He finally recognized it, and believing that Jacobsen must still be flying it he began screaming curses and abuse at his former partner. He jerked the wheel left, then right, then left again, skewering across the sky. And when he levelled out Lima One was still hovering above him. He had to drop lower, and now he was dangerously close to the wild, rock-strewn slopes below.

'I gotta go down,' he yelled fearfully. 'I gotta find a place and put us down.'

'No!' Kitaka shrieked at him. His face was now grey with fear and his eyes rolled like huge, red-veined marbles, but he wasn't giving up. 'We nearly there, man. Just keep going. We must be nearly there.'

'I gotta go down,' Kyller repeated. 'That crazy bastard's gonna wreck us for sure.'

'Then get out from under him.' Kitaka was jerking his neck from side to side as he squirmed in his seat for a clear view of the remorseless steel nemesis behind them. He was hugging his AK-47 close to his chest and his frustration, like Kyller's terror, was a thick choking thing in his throat.

'Get out from under him!' he bawled again. 'Let me get a shot.'

'I can't,' Kyller groaned. He had realized that he was beaten and had virtually given up trying. The man he believed to be Jacobsen was too good for him. Lima One had the edge and he couldn't escape. And while Lima One stayed right on top of them Kitaka couldn't use the rifle. Kyller had stopped him the first time he had tried, pointing out that to try and fire through the sweep of their own rotors would only shoot off the blades and cause them to crash. While the other pilot could maintain his top dog position he was using their rotors as a shield.

Kyller became resigned to the inevitable and looked for a place to land. The mountains had reared up again on his right and for the moment there was nowhere. Then Kitaka gave a sudden shout of elation.

'There!' He had seen the looming outline of a peak he recognized. 'That's it. We made it. Turn away from the mountains and follow the river.'

For a moment Kyller couldn't see any river. Then abruptly it was there, a rushing swirl of black water spilling down from the heights. He turned thankfully to follow it down to lower, and hopefully more level ground.

Beside him Kitaka was grinning. He knew where he was now. The river was the Black Umfolozi, its course winding down through the vast Umfolozi Wilderness, one of the last unspoiled, untamed areas of southern Africa. It was also part of what had been Zululand, the tribal homeland of Nicholas Temela. And somewhere down there, waiting with a truck, was a group of Temela's friends.

'Put her down first place you see,' Kitaka ordered. 'When you do I'll run out clear of our blades and shoot down that crazy man behind us.'

He was too confused to find the exact rendezvous, but he was confident they were close enough for the Zulus to hear the noise and come running.

Falcon could see that Kyller was looking for a place to land, and so he held back, still keeping his ten o'clock high position, but no longer pushing the risk of a collision. He saw a flat stretch of stony but otherwise clear riverbank coming up ahead and hovered as Lima Two settled down toward it.

In that moment Kyller took a last, desperate gamble.

Kyller had realized that the other pilot was holding back, and suddenly he was as scared of what might happen after they had landed as he had previously been of a mid-air crash. Suddenly, urgently, he wanted to take his own fate into his own hands, and in a flare of temper he knew that this was his last chance to show Jacobsen a winning trick.

He had been moving down to land, but then he gunned the engine to full power, made a sharp, twisting turn and shot upward. If he had made the surprise climb successfully he could have reversed their positions — but he didn't make it.

Falcon had almost relaxed, thinking that Kyller's nerve had broken and their fantastic and gruelling duel was over. Then Lima Two surged upward. Kyller was twisting left. Falcon had no choice but to twist right or Kyller's blades would have sliced right through the cabin windows of Lima One.

Helen screamed as the blur of steel slashed close. Then the two helicopters were moving apart but still climbing fast. Kyller had the advantage of momentum but then the tips of the rotor blades touched as the machines were passing.

There was a terrific double bang as both sets of rotor blades shattered, and both helicopters spun helplessly out of control.

The blades on Lima Two disintegrated totally. Kyller felt the machine drop beneath him, hurtling downward with stomach-sickening speed. Mercifully they were close to earth and it was only seconds to impact. The machine thumped down with a bone-jarring jolt and skidded forward. Then the landing skids buckled and collapsed and she tilted sideways.

Lima One was still airborne with half a rotor blade still whirling, but she was making a curling nosedive toward an outcrop of massive black boulders a hundred yards further on down the riverbank. Falcon yelled at Helen to jump and there was just enough time for both of them to unbuckle their quick-release safety belts and throw back the sliding doors on either side of the cabin.

Falcon gave Helen a push to help her out, and then dived from the opposite side. They both left the cabin while the helicopter was still skimming to destruction at a height of twenty feet above the river. They fell hard into the shallows where the river curved and there was just enough water to break their fall.

Then Lima One struck the rocks and exploded in a thunderclap of red fire.

The explosion stunned them and the shock wave of disturbed water threw up their bodies onto a strip of sand beach where they lay unconscious and half-drowned.

CHAPTER 12

Mike Kyller was numb and dazed. His fingers fumbled in slow motion to release his seat belt and with an effort he pushed himself upright, away from the tilted angle of the cabin door. He was aware of Jonas Kitaka hanging limp in his straps slightly above and beside him, but for a moment he could only stare in horror at the blazing fireball of Lima One further down the river.

He had seen the two bodies fall clear and was still under the mistaken belief that one of them must be Jacobsen. In his present shock-bewildered state of mind he didn't know whether he hated Jacobsen as an enemy, or still owed him a debt as a friend, but he felt an urgent need to discover whether the man was alive or dead.

While Kyller struggled to slide back the cabin door and get out, Kitaka blinked and opened his eyes.

Kyller got the door half open. With the helicopter slumped over to one side there was only just enough room for him to crawl out between the stony ground and the edge of the cabin roof. He got clear on his knees and then straightened up and began to stumble forward.

Kitaka's hand pulled at his shoulder and stopped him.

'Where the hell you going, man?'

Kyller turned and looked into the hostile eyes.

'Jacobsen,' he faltered. 'He could be alive.'

'Then we'll finish him later,' Kitaka snarled. 'Right now we gotta get this thing out before our chopper catches fire.'

The thing was the huge, finned artillery shell. Kyller had temporarily forgotten their stolen cargo, but now he looked back and saw that it had slipped over the rear seats and was jammed against the half-open door. His stomach turned to jelly and he was almost sick as he remembered the metallic banging and scraping as he had forced the door back. He had been bashing the door against the sharp nose of the shell.

In the same moment he became aware of the pressing reasons for Kitaka's urgency. The strong smell of leaking petrol from the ruptured fuel lines of Lima Two, and the fiery heat radiating from the already burning Lima One. It could only be a matter of seconds before a spark ignited the spreading mist of petrol vapour, and Lima Two would become a second inferno.

Kyller almost fainted with fear, and began to back off. His legs were too weak to run. Kitaka grabbed his reluctant ally by the shirt-front and held him. He was still holding his AK-47 and he rammed the muzzle into Kyller's cringing belly. Kitaka had got this far and he didn't intend to lose his precious victory now.

'You help me, Sergeant Mike,' he spat viciously. 'You help me, or I kill you now.'

He didn't give Kyller time to argue and pushed the South African back toward the helicopter. Kyller's shoulders hit the edge of the cabin roof and he was pinned there by the rifle. There was no mercy in Kitaka's face and Kyller knew he had no choice. He turned and dropped on his knees, choking on his own terror and the stink of petrol as he reached into the open door to pull at the shiny steel casing. Kitaka slung the AK-47 over one shoulder and crawled into the doorway to help.

Together they dragged the thing clear, getting their arms around it and hugging it to their chests as they staggered back under the weight. It had taken four men to lift it on board, but feeling the heat on their backs and knowing the helicopter could blow up at any second gave them the strength of desperation.

Kyller had the nose and Kitaka the end with the tail fins, and gasping and straining they carried it upriver along the bank. After fifty yards Kyller tripped over a large tuft of grass and fell sideways. The shell rolled on top of him as Kitaka skipped clear.

In the same second the petrol vapour leaking from Lima Two ignited. The blast of the explosion swept over them and when they looked back both helicopters were burning.

They rested, too exhausted to move any further, and five minutes later Kitaka's friends found them.

An ancient, much-battered pick-up truck rattled out of the dark bush to the north and braked in a swirl of dust. Kitaka greeted the four Africans who climbed out with exchanges of backslapping and laughter, but then he made the effort to curb his relief and postpone the detailed story-swapping until later. He began giving orders again and the prize he had captured from the South African air base was quickly loaded onto the back of the truck.

Kyller watched, too bruised and weakened to make any move, and when Kitaka came back to him he knew it was the end. He felt no surprise when the AK-47 was again pointed at his stomach, just disgust with himself, and the feeling that he deserved what was coming.

'So long, Sergeant Mike.' Now the pressure was off Kitaka's grin was casual, without malice. 'This is where we were meant to part anyway.'

Kitaka squeezed the trigger and Kyller died, his body hammered bloodily into the dust. For a moment he stood to admire his handiwork, then he shrugged, spat as though to clear his throat of a bad taste, and turned away.

There was still no time to waste, and within another minute the truck and the five black Africans had disappeared from the scene.

Dawn was clawing with red fingers over the shadowed bush to the east when Falcon slowly recovered consciousness. He was lying face down on the edge of the river, his shoulders dry and his feet trailing in the water. He opened one eye, the other was pressed against sharp gravel, and then painfully raised his head. He saw he was midway between two dying fires, which were the smouldering wrecks of the two burned-out helicopters.

He had a splitting headache, and his whole body felt as though he had been pounded from head to foot with a large hammer. He tentatively moved each limb in turn, fully expecting a shaft of splintered agony, but nothing was broken.

Slowly he pushed himself to his knees and sat up. He swayed dizzily and there was blood crusted over his left eye. He picked it away with his fingers, felt for the cut above it, and suddenly remembered Helen.

He found her close beside him, sprawled on her back, her face bruised and gravel-scratched, and her hair flung out in a golden halo on the sand. He crawled over to her and ran his hands gently over her body, checking each limb in turn. He could feel no breaks, and no stickiness of blood, and began to hope that she too had escaped lightly.

His shirt was in shreds and he pulled off a sleeve that had already started to come apart at the seam. He used it to bathe Helen's face, and after ten minutes she blinked open her eyes.

He helped her to stand and she leaned against him for support as they stared at what remained of the two helicopters. Then slowly they began to take note of the wilderness around them.

After five minutes they spotted the crumpled heap that was Kyller and limped toward it. Ants and butterflies were sipping peacefully at the spilled pools of Kyller's blood, although the vultures and the bigger scavengers had not yet spotted the potential feast. Falcon looked around and read the story of what had happened in the footprints and tyre marks on the dusty earth.

'Poor Mike,' Helen said with a shudder.

'Poor Mike,' Falcon echoed. 'Poor Jacobsen. Poor Lena.' And as a bitter afterthought. 'Poor bloody Judy.'

They moved further up the river, far enough to escape the smell, but remaining close enough to hurl stones to keep the vultures away from the corpse. There they sat side by side, silently waiting.

An hour passed before a police helicopter found them. It was searching in response to Helen's brief radio broadcast, and on board was a furious Colonel Weissner. Falcon had never before seen any man in such a towering, apoplectic, and totally impotent rage.

By the time Weissner had located the scene of the double helicopter crash Jonas Kitaka had again succeeded in giving himself a substantial lead. It was enough to find the nearest tarmac road to the north and drive the last hundred miles to the Natal coast. There, in a small, secluded estuary, a fast motor launch was waiting to take him on the last lap of his long, roundabout journey to the safety of friendly Mozambique.

The sea was dazzling under the hot blue sky as Kitaka climbed on board. The boat was a sportsman's craft, the paintwork gleaming white, and the woodwork dark polished teak. He was welcomed by more gleeful friends, and one silent stranger.

The stranger was not an African, at least, not a black African. His skin was light brown in colour, and there was a hawk nose on his strong, handsome face. He was seated in a fisherman's chair in the rear of the boat, and he slowly reeled in his line and put his rod to one side. He waited until the exuberant reunions were complete and then stepped forward, facing Kitaka for the first time.

'I should not be here,' he said calmly, his voice only slightly critical. 'But your friends insisted I must come. They are afraid of what you are bringing on board. They wish me to examine it and assure them it is safe.' He smiled and offered a firm hand. 'I am Salem Sharif.'

For a moment Kitaka was blank and baffled, but then he understood. This must be the Libyan technical expert he had been promised by the Russians. A grin split the thick black bush of his beard and he took the offered hand and tried to crush it in his powerful grasp.

Sharif did not flinch. Instead he continued in the same tone: 'As I am here I thought it would be wise to provide us all with a logical cover. This is a tourist area for fishing and waterskiing, so a boat with a man playing at sea-fishing will not arouse any suspicion.'

Kitaka nodded approval, even though he was annoyed that he could not crack the knuckles of the hand. He released it, still grinning.

'I am Jonas Kitaka,' he announced proudly. 'I am the leader of the *Black K Liberation Army.*'

Sharif inclined his head slightly in formal acknowledgement. 'Were you successful in your recent mission?' he enquired.

Kitaka nodded. They weighed each other for another moment with calculating eyes, and then the African turned and shouted for his men to bring on board the proof.

Sharif watched the task being performed in resumed silence. He had found his future ally, but not a friend, for all he could see was a cold, cruel man he instinctively did not trust.

For his part Kitaka had seen another essential tool, to be used as needed, and then discarded without remorse when that usefulness was over. To Kitaka, Salem Sharif was just another Mike Kyller.

Falcon had expected that he and Helen would be returned to Johannesburg, but he was mistaken. Instead they were flown directly to the outskirts of Pretoria, where a fast car was waiting to take them into the centre of the administrative capital. Their final destination was a modern eleven-storey block on Skinner Street, outwardly no different to the other high-rise office blocks in the city, except for the large radio antenna on its roof.

Inside the entrances and reception areas were monitored by remote-controlled TV cameras, and there was one-way glass in all the doors with unrestricted vision from the centre of the building outwards.

Weissner was no longer bothering with any pretence of his role. He had brought them back to BOSS Headquarters, where it was soon obvious that he was a very senior officer in Division B, the department responsible for dealing with subversion.

Falcon and Helen retold their story again and again. They were not disbelieved, but their interrogators had the faces of haunted and desperate men. The building around them was a turmoil of feverish activity, and it was obvious that Weissner and all his colleagues were under terrific pressure from above.

By the end of the day the red-necked Colonel had to concede that somehow Jonas Kitaka had escaped. And Falcon had also guessed at the object of the daring and successful raid on the air base.

Through his association with Killian, Falcon had virtually free access to all MI5 and other British Intelligence agency files, and he knew that the South Africans had long been suspected of developing an independent nuclear capability.

In June 1977 both US and Soviet spy satellites had observed preparations for a nuclear test in a remote area of the Kalahari desert. The South Africans had withdrawn from the attempt when they realized the Kalahari site was no longer secret, but two years later another US satellite had recorded two bright flashes far out in the South Atlantic off the Cape of Good Hope.

It was believed that a South African warship had fired two tactical nuclear warheads contained in large, long-range artillery shells.

There was also evidence that the South African Atomic Energy Board had drawn up maps of their northern borders, showing the safe areas where tactical atomic weapons could be used without causing any serious seismic damage, or affecting any major white population areas.

If the capability existed then it was logical to assume that the weapons would be stored at major front-line military bases like Hoedspruit.

Falcon put his suspicion to Weissner and the South African harshly and emphatically denied it. But all his blustering rage could not hide the stark fear which lay behind the hard grey eyes.

Falcon knew then, without any shadow of doubt, that Jonas Kitaka and his *Black K* organization had succeeded in stealing an atomic warhead.

CHAPTER 13

Ten days passed before Falcon was allowed to leave South Africa. Helen accompanied him on the short flight north to Salisbury in neighbouring Zimbabwe. There they joined the twenty-strong group of international press men and women who boarded the privately chartered short-range jet which took them out to the Project *Vulcan* launch site in Mozambique.

Their first glimpse of the launch area was from the air. It was an approximately diamond-shaped network of roads, carved out of the virgin thorn scrub and jungle in the heart of the remote Sul Do Save province. A runway had been built at the western end of the diamond, jutting out into the thick bush, and Falcon recalled that the site was supposed to be virtually inaccessible except from the air. Looking down from the passenger cabin window of the press corps jet it was possible to believe it.

Grouped in the southern point of the diamond was a cluster of solid brick and concrete buildings, which proved to be the administration and accommodation blocks, together with the launch control centre. In the northern point of the diamond were the storage sheds, with the liquid fuel store even further isolated from the rest.

The actual launch pad was at the extreme eastern tip of the diamond, with a rocket already standing erect beside the black, steel-web tower of its maintenance platforms.

The map showed 6,000 square miles of uninhabited country between the nearest marked roads and the main railway line between Zimbabwe and the Indian Ocean which passed forty miles to the south of the launch site. A further forty miles to the south the map showed the South African border, the same border which formed the northern perimeter of the Kruger Game Park.

From there, as Falcon well knew, it was only a few hours' drive to the major cities of Pretoria and Johannesburg.

The jet landed and taxied toward the control tower at the eastern end of the runway. There the mixed assortment of press representatives were packed into two minibuses and driven the last quarter mile to the administration complex. At this point the young press officer who had accompanied them from Salisbury introduced them to Herr Gunter Hauptmann, the Administrative Director for Project *Vulcan*.

Hauptmann was a short, heavy, bullet-headed man in his mid-fifties. He had been born in East Berlin, combining a hard pragmatism with a stolid strength of character that had enabled him to build a major industrial empire out of the rubble and the ruins. There were many who failed to understand why Hauptmann had not fled to the West to employ his talents, like so many of his contemporaries. But perhaps Hauptmann's special talent was that he could work and build hand in glove with the usually damaging pressures of state control. The fact remained that the East German aeronautical company, of which he was the driving force, was one of the most successful industrial and technological enterprises in the Eastern Bloc.

He gave them a prepared speech of welcome, playing his role as host with cheerful enthusiasm. The next item on the agenda was a three-course meal, with cold beer or chilled wine served as desired. Afterwards they were shown to the newly constructed guest huts they would occupy for the forty-eight hours of their planned visit.

The huts were clean, white-walled, thatch-roofed rondavels, similar to those found in game parks and outdoor tourist centres throughout southern Africa. They formed a neat circle and each one accommodated two reporters. Falcon and Helen chose the one which was nearest to the control centre and the launch pad.

Finally, when all the needs of human comfort had been catered for, the press group assembled again beside the minibuses for an extensive tour of the facility. Hauptmann joined them again as their host and guide, but this time he brought the added support of two of his key personnel.

'Permit me to introduce Doctor Theodore Praeger, and Herr Max Koslowski.' He indicated each man in turn with a wave of his hand. 'Doctor Praeger is a scientist and our Technical Director. The design and function of Project *Vulcan* is mostly his own creative work. Max is our Security Chief. He was previously a sergeant major in the East German Army.'

Praeger smiled an acknowledgement and bowed slightly. He was a thin man with receding whisps of grey hair and plain, rimless spectacles. A slim calculator jutted from one breast pocket of his crisp white coat, and the other was filled with a range of pens and pencils.

Falcon knew he had worked in a minor capacity with Von Braun during World War Two, and he was one of the few who had not been snapped up by either the Americans or the Russians at the war's end. Then he had not been important enough, but he had persevered over the years and continued to develop his interest and knowledge in the fields of space technology and rocketry.

Killian had not been able to provide Falcon with any advance knowledge on Koslowski. The Security Chief was a tough, ugly-looking man who had at some time suffered a broken jaw which had healed with a peculiar twist. He clicked his heels and squared his shoulders as he was introduced, which was in keeping with a military background.

A slim, middle-aged African wearing a white shirt and blue suit was hovering on the edge of the group. Hauptmann motioned him forward and added diplomatically:

'And this is Doctor Olenga, who represents the government of Mozambique. We are deeply indebted to Doctor Olenga, and to his government in Maputo, for granting us permission to establish our facility here, and for all the cooperation and assistance we have received.'

Olenga beamed. He had a round face and perfect white teeth. 'Mozambique is very happy to help Project *Vulcan*. This is a joint enterprise between a leading Marxist-Socialist country of Europe and the leading Marxist-Socialist country of Africa. We shall launch many peaceful satellites, and our triumph will be the triumph of international Marxist-Socialism.'

Hauptmann's frown was just noticeable. Either he didn't want political speeches, or he had prepared something better for his own chosen time.

'My colleagues will be able to answer any of your questions which I may find difficult,' the senior director promised smoothly. 'But first we will tour the facility and show you exactly what is happening here. There will be plenty of time for all your questions afterward.'

There were a few ruffled feathers among the journalists, most of whom were already bursting with questions, but Hauptmann turned quickly to his jeep which was to lead the small convoy around the site. The press corps piled into their minibuses and followed its swirling dust cloud out to the launch pad.

The rocket was a vertical white pencil of steel, six feet in diameter, only slightly flared at the base where the engines were housed, and almost one hundred feet in height. It was a two-stage vehicle and the name *Vulcan* was painted in vertical red letters on the lower stage. The sharpened nose cone was in position, although technicians were still working at that level on the upper platform of the maintenance tower.

Hauptmann gave another brief set speech on the dimensions, thrust, range, and other technical data of the rocket, but the same information had been given on the printed handout they had all been invited to read on the flight from Salisbury, so Falcon only partially listened. Instead he was more interested in looking at the rocket. It was, he decided, a close copy of the Soviet two-stage small Cosmos satellite launcher which had hurled up the bulk of the Soviet Union's research instruments during the sixties. Now updated and superseded by the huge Soyuz and Proton launch vehicles which carried space stations and manned space capsules the comparatively puny Cosmos model was still a well-tried and proven design for putting up small satellite payloads.

Praeger answered the short barrage of immediate questions, and then Hauptmann got what Helen had already christened 'the scribbler's circus' moving again. The jeep and the minibuses circled the launch pad, with cameras clicking at every possible angle, and then headed out to the storage areas. On the way they passed the huge steel-web discs of the two radar tracking stations.

Again Hauptmann made the introduction, and then Praeger answered specific questions. There were body sections, engines and components sufficient to construct two more launch vehicles already on site, so Praeger was able to describe the function of each piece of equipment in turn. He was nervous, obviously unaccustomed to so much publicity, and sometimes flustered by too many questions at once. At the same time it was clear he knew his own brainchild in total depth, and without the constant interruptions shifting him from one track to another he would have been happy to talk for hours on end.

The tour was finally concluded at the launch control centre, where the first note of sourness marked the proceedings. Hauptmann had embarked upon a detailed explanation of the computer banks and data screens and proudly described them as electronic marvels of purely East German design. To which a disgusted Frenchman from the circus muttered darkly and none-too-softly, 'Pah, it is industrial espionage!'

Hauptmann scowled, faltered for a second, and then chose to ignore the remark. He finished what he had been saying, and then went on without pause for questions:

'We have shown you everything there is to see, here at Project *Vulcan*, so now I must explain to you why we are here, and what we hope to achieve. The rocket you have seen on the launch pad we have designated *Vulcan One*. Except for the final task of fuelling, which will take place tomorrow morning, it is all ready to be fired into space. Countdown will conclude at noon tomorrow when the rocket will launch our first satellite into fixed orbit above Central Africa.'

He moved to a full-sized model, a sphere some four feet in diameter with four slender, telescopic antenna, which stood on a table at the rear of the control room.

'This is the type of satellite which *Vulcan One* will take into space, a telecommunications satellite which will help to revolutionise radio and television communications throughout Africa. It will be a beginning, gentlemen, a first step to sharing the vast benefits of modern space technology with the peoples of Africa and the Third World.'

'Are you serious?' an American reporter asked. 'Do you really expect to put a TV set in every mud hut along the Congo and the Zambezi?'

'Why not?' Hauptmann demanded calmly. 'The world satellite television market is already valued in millions of dollars per year and is constantly expanding. Until recently only the US and Soviet governments had the capability to launch rockets, but now the commercial field has opened up and is visibly growing. The European Space Centre in French Guiana has launched three rockets in their attempts to capture a slice of this market. The West German company OTRAG are making their effort from their new launch site in Libya. Here at Project *Vulcan* we see no reason why this potentially vast and profitable area of modern technology should become the sole monopoly of America and Europe. We intend to secure our share of future markets in space.'

'Then the purpose of *Vulcan* is not entirely humanitarian.' The American seemed to think he had scored a point.

'There will be benefits for everybody,' Hauptmann said patiently. 'Just as any manufacturer's products will only sell as long as they are of benefit to the consumer. But if you are accusing me of running a perfectly viable commercial company which is expected to show a fair rate of return on our not inconsiderable investment, then I must plead guilty.' He paused to smile. 'It is a sin we have learned from the Americans.'

He won a few faint chuckles, then the Frenchman asked bluntly:

'What about its military potential?'

'Project *Vulcan* has no military potential.' It was the question Hauptmann had been waiting for and he dealt it a flat denial. 'Our activities here in Mozambique are entirely peaceful in intention. As I have already explained, our main interest is in the growing demand for telecommunications, but we will be prepared to launch weather-observation satellites, and any kind of peaceful satellite payload our future customers may bring to us.'

'Does that include spy satellites?'

Hauptmann shook his head. 'We do not wish to be involved with that kind of payload. That is a government-level policy decision, and also the personal wish of myself and Doctor Praeger.'

The Frenchman and a small hardcore of sceptics would not let the issue rest, and the argument continued at a lively pace. Praeger joined Hauptmann in repeated denials that their rocket could be converted to any military use, and both men insisted again and again that the planned operations of Project *Vulcan* were entirely peaceful. They foresaw sufficient demand for commercial payload flights to keep their facility busy, without even having to consider the borderline ethics of spy satellites.

An oblique suggestion that the unqualified support of the host government might have sinister undertones brought an indignant response from Olenga. His government, he claimed, would *never* attempt to subvert Project *Vulcan* to any form of military function. As good Marxist-Socialists his government believed in equality for all peoples, which meant an equal share in the fruits of advanced space technology. And in the short term, he stressed emphatically, the revenues from the ground rent for the facility would be used to finance a revolutionary new program of Marxist-Socialist advancement for his country.

Listening to them Falcon formed the opinion that they were all sincere, and that all three believed implicitly in what they were saying. Their hearts were honest, their intentions were good.

And the road to hell was paved with good intentions.

Falcon was equally sure they had been set up. Behind the scenes the Mozambique government had been duped, and the directors of *Vulcan* were unknowing and expendable figureheads.

Falcon and Helen had both refrained from making themselves too noticeable, knowing that every possible question would eventually get asked and answered, and it was a West German journalist who finally voiced their fears.

'Herr Hauptmann,' he began. 'You must know that this is a politically volatile part of Africa. Also we live in a world that is continually shocked by the violence of international terrorism. Therefore, how can you be sure that your facility is not vulnerable to outside attack?'

'A highly imaginative idea.' Hauptmann smiled to show he did not take it seriously. 'There is nothing here of value to terrorists because the *Vulcan* rocket does not have a military warhead. But this is a security question, so I will let Max answer it.'

Koslowski had been standing silent in the background. Now he cleared his throat and said forcefully: 'You have perhaps noticed the ten-foot-high perimeter fence surrounding the facility. It was erected to prevent wild animals from straying inside, but it is electrified and will serve equally well to deter any human attack. Also I have thirty-six armed guards under my command. Twelve guards will be on duty at all times, at the airfield control tower, the launch control centre, and patrolling the other areas. The twenty-four men at rest are on immediate call.'

He shrugged his shoulders and added: 'These precautions are routine, but almost certainly unnecessary. We are so remote from the nearest track or footpath that only an air attack could hope to capture this facility. The terrorists would have to drop by parachute, and in force, and even the best equipped terrorists simply do not have these resources.'

'In Mozambique such a thing could not happen.' Olenga had to have the last prim word. 'We have a stable Marxist-Socialist government. Our country is safe and secure. There can be no need for invited guests to concern themselves.'

The debate went on until Hauptmann wound it up with a promise that they would all have the opportunity to ask more questions later. In the meantime he and Praeger had urgent work to ensure that the countdown stayed on schedule.

Most of the journalists rested through the heat of the afternoon. In the evening another first-class meal was provided, and afterwards they were able to mix socially with the *Vulcan* directors, technicians and other personnel. A great deal of alcohol was consumed at Hauptmann's expense, and by the end of the evening it had all developed into a relaxed and noisy party.

Falcon and Helen were among the first to leave, followed by knowing leers and winks from some of Falcon's more jealous male contemporaries. They returned to their guest hut and there Helen undressed as casually as though they had been married for years. She rolled onto one of the beds and lay back naked, waiting.

Falcon had drank sparingly throughout the evening. He was cold sober and stood by the window, staring out thoughtfully at the tall silhouette of the rocket. It was half a mile distant on its launch pad, and held a dramatic, symmetrical beauty in the moonlight.

Helen sensed his mood. She lit a cigarette, exhaled smoke, and said quietly, 'You think it will be tonight.'

Falcon nodded. 'Tonight that rocket is all ready for launching. By this time tomorrow it will have burned out in space and they'll have to wait months for another one to be assembled. Plus if they can take the facility while the circus is here they can get maximum publicity. If what we expect to happen is going to happen, then it has to be tonight.'

'You've warned Koslowski? I saw you get him to one side halfway through the evening.'

'I tried,' Falcon said wryly. 'I pointed out that the moment was ripe for any terrorists who might have the idea in mind, and tactfully suggested that he strengthened his security patrols. But our friend Max is still convinced that *Vulcan* is invincible except from the air. He scoffed politely and told me not to worry.'

Helen was worried and tried to be optimistic. '*Vulcan* will be a tough nut to crack.'

'So was Hoedspruit,' Falcon reminded her.

Helen sighed, sat up and reached for her underclothes.

'Okay,' she said. 'I'm getting dressed again. The night promises to be full of action, and it doesn't look as though any of it is going to happen in bed.'

CHAPTER 14

The attack came just before dawn, and it was even more devastating and efficient than Falcon had feared. It was also the kind of attack which Koslowski had believed impossible, and against which he had no adequate defence.

The first spearhead came from the air.

It came in the form of two MiG-7 fighter aircraft which hurtled out of the night darkness from the north. They streaked low over the facility and at point-blank range fired clusters of wing rockets at their chosen targets. The first direct hit was on the airfield control tower which exploded outward in a blast of red flame. The two-man tower control team and two of Koslowski's guards who were inside were killed instantly.

The number two MiG was only seconds behind the leader. Its target was the long accommodation block which housed the bulk of Koslowski's off-duty security force. Two missiles smashed through the roof and exploded inside the building. Gouts of red fire flashed upward and the weakened roof collapsed. More than half of the men inside were killed or crushed in their beds. Those who survived and managed to crawl out of the burning rubble were too shocked, stunned or injured to put up any effective fight.

The jets turned and came screaming back at low level on their second run. This time they used cannon fire to hammer the remaining buildings in the accommodation and administration area. They spared only the separate bungalows of the senior directors, the guest huts sheltering the journalists, and the vital launch control centre which was needed intact.

With the lower rank and file of *Vulcan* personnel they were merciless.

On their second run in the jets also used the last of their rockets to blast gaps through the electrified perimeter fence. Through the long hours of darkness Jonas Kitaka had led a handpicked force of one hundred *Black K* guerrillas through the last ten miles of unmapped bush and jungle to encircle the launch site, and now they stormed through the shattered defences.

They had been divided into ten-man squads, the spearhead groups led by Kitaka and Nicholas Temela. Many of them wore hooded masks, a morale-cracking device learned from more sophisticated terrorist groups, and intended to make them look more fearsome.

Each squad had a specific task. One to secure the rocket on its launch pad, another to secure the storage area, others to mop up around the administration blocks.

Kitaka was intent on capturing the senior technicians alive. He knew he would need them. Temela's key role was to take the launch control centre.

They were all armed with the deadly AK-47 combat rifles, and they had all been carefully schooled in the Moscow-controlled terrorist training camps to the north. They were the best underground army black Africa could produce, and with their objective softened up in advance by the air attack they were supremely confident.

They rushed into battle with speed and determination, yelling their tribal war cries as they shot their way bloodily through the last handful of Koslowski's guards.

The security boss had been sleeping in one of the private bungalows reserved for senior personnel. He awoke to the startling sound of cannon fire and explosions and tumbled out of bed. He grabbed for his trousers and a submachine gun and ran out into the flaming night.

The entire complex seemed to be on fire and there were men screaming and running in all directions. The roaring shadow of a MiG thundered over his head and he ducked and fell flat on his face. He got up quickly, cursing and shaking his fist at the sky.

He began to run then, heading for the accommodation block to rally his men. When he saw it in ruins and burning fiercely he stopped. It was as though he had run into a brick wall of shock and momentarily he was sickened.

From behind the main administration block to his left he heard the vicious crackle of automatic rifle fire. He realized the facility was being attacked at ground level from that direction, and for a moment he was torn between the demand of duty, and the pitiful screams for help from his burned, maimed and dying men.

But Max Koslowski had been a sergeant major in the East German Army. Until now he had taken his duties lightly, keeping a firm check on pilfering by the native workforce during the site construction stage, and believing that there would be nothing more serious to bother him. Now the crunch was here and he gathered himself together and showed what he was made of. He was a tough leader, a man of grit and guts, and he had the military discipline necessary to get his priorities in the right order. He turned his back on the fiery scene of death and carnage and ran to intercept the ground attack.

On the way he collided with one of his two-man security patrols and yelled at them to follow him. The two men obeyed and turned to run at his heels. Like Koslowski they were armed with submachine guns.

They turned the corner of the administration block and faced the first wave of *Black K*. The two sides exchanged fire and Koslowski bawled at his two men to hit the ground as the terrorists began to diverge and scatter. He saw several of the enemy fall, but in the same second one of his own men gagged and died as a bullet ripped through his throat.

Still urging on the survivor Koslowski began to wriggle forward. He knew it was hopeless, the sheer weight of numbers in front of him was too many, but he continued to blaze away with the submachine gun.

Fifty yards in front of Koslowski, Jonas Kitaka had been forced to throw himself flat on the earth. He too wriggled swiftly forward. On either side of him the men of his squad were blazing away with their combat rifles, and drawing all the return fire from the two defenders. Kitaka was too experienced to let a red flash of muzzle flame betray his own position. In this situation he preferred to use one of the two hand grenades clipped to his belt. He pulled the pin with his teeth and threw it forward.

The grenade came to a bouncing, rolling stop only six inches from Koslowski's nose as he lay on his belly on the dry grass. For one frozen millisecond of time the doomed man stared at it with wide, mesmerized eyes. And then, before he could roll away, it blew up in his face.

Falcon had been standing by the open window of the rondavel, smoking a cigarette from the slowly depleting packet of Dunhill's in his breast pocket. Helen was dozing on the nearest bed. They had taken it in turns to catnap after the facility had settled down for the night.

He had guessed that Kitaka would want to take the journalists alive, so when the jets had attacked he had snapped at Helen to stay in the guest hut. She sat bolt upright, staring at him, but he didn't wait to see whether she intended to obey. He vaulted over the windowsill and headed fast for open ground.

Once clear he stopped, crouching low and pausing to take stock of what was happening. He had to read Kitaka's battle plan quickly before he could make any counter-plan of his own.

A glance to his right showed that the airfield control tower had been obliterated. It was a quarter of a mile away but the flames there were high and bright. The jets had struck so suddenly that he doubted whether the duty crew in the control room would have had any chance to transmit a radio call for help.

The accommodation block was also an inferno, and he felt a moment of pity for Koslowski and his security forces. Their soft life, and their feeling of invulnerability had been short-lived.

The fighter planes were returning for their second strike, and this time Falcon recognized their short, stubby silhouette. He had seen MiG-17s in action before and the chopped-off nose and the large, back slanted tail fins were unmistakcable.

He threw himself flat as the Migs howled overhead, and despite the deafening pounding of their cannon fire he strained to identify the colouring and lettering on the fuselage. Both planes were blurred by speed and darkness, but he thought he could recognize the markings of the Mozambique Air Force.

Falcon scrambled to his feet again. Now the jets had passed he could identify another familiar sound, the spiteful crackle of Kalashnikov AK-47s bursting through the perimeter fence.

Falcon felt the old combat thrill taking over his nerves and instincts. His brain was ice-cold, calculating fast, and it was obvious that the facility had no hope of holding out against such a massive and cold-blooded attack. Project *Vulcan* would be totally under terrorist control within a very short space of time, so the only useful course of action he could follow now would be to get a warning to the outside world.

The airfield control tower was gone. There was a radio in the press corps jet which had been parked at the far end of the runway, but that was almost three-quarters of a mile away. The only other radio equipment would be in the launch control centre, an obvious priority target for the terrorists, but much closer to hand.

Falcon began to run. The MiGs had ignored the control centre and Koslowski should have a few of his guards posted there. With luck they could hold the centre long enough to use the radio. It was the only hope left that was worth a try.

He realized immediately it was a three-way race. Himself, a squad of terrorists running in from the surrounding bush, and a short, bullet-headed figure who had stumbled out of one of the executive bungalows ahead of him.

Hauptmann seemed to have the same idea. He was sprinting for the control building wearing nothing but his white undershorts. They made a clear if moving target in the moonlight and a burst of automatic fire chased after him and cut him down.

Falcon had been moving low, he was dressed in dark clothing and the nearest of the bungalows still screened him from the advancing terrorists. He threw himself flat beside a low garden wall, cursing because he was unarmed and too late, and watched Temela's squad closing in on the control centre.

Koslowski had three guards there. They knocked out the windows and put up a desperate last-ditch fight, forcing the big Zulu and his men to scatter and take ground cover. Falcon saw one of the terrorists fall and heard him screaming as he writhed on the ground in pain. Temela paid no heed to the fallen man but tongue-lashed his faltering men into a renewed advance. They squirmed forward on their bellies, firing as they went.

Falcon changed direction and ran to the man who had been hit. The African was rolling from side to side on his back, whimpering now as he clasped both hands to his belly. Blood was spurting through his fingers and he was too far gone to know that Falcon had paused briefly beside him to pick up his dropped AK-47.

During his extensive military training Falcon had become expert with every type of Western small arms, and with most of the Eastern Bloc weapons as well. Also, on several of the terrorist battlefields to which he had been directed by Killian, he had become exceptionally proficient with the Kalashnikov. This was not the first time he had armed himself with a weapon taken from the enemy, and it was always the same weapon. The AK-47 was almost an old friend.

The Falcon ran on. He was now behind Temela and his ten-man squad and they were concentrating their fire on the launch control centre. Falcon got close, within twenty yards, before the nearest terrorist heard the fast swish of his feet through the grass. The man started to turn, his eyeballs popping, his mouth opening to shout. Falcon fired and the African died as the burst of bullets ripped through his chest.

Falcon kept on firing, slashing the AK-47 from left to right across his body and cutting down the terrorists in front of him. Half of Temela's spearhead squad died in those few swift, bloody seconds of time. They fell screaming and the others rolled for cover.

Temela had survived. He was ahead of his men and it was the rear rank who had died. The big Zulu realized he was caught in a crossfire and turned to deal with the threat from behind. He saw only one flashing gun muzzle and with a roar of fury he charged to meet it.

It was the fearless, death-defying charge his ancestors had made at Isandlwana where the Zulu warriors had slaughtered the British in 1879. It might have succeeded again, for many men would have faltered in the face of such suicidal ferocity. But this time his opponent was no ordinary man.

As Falcon had finished his murderous scything action he had veered off to the right, thrown himself flat, rolled over twice, and came to rest in a prone firing position ready to chop down new targets. Temela had charged the spot where he had been, and by the time the big Zulu had changed direction the Falcon had his weapon levelled again. Temela was firing from the hip and his bullets thudded into the earth beside Falcon's elbow, hurling dirt and grass into Falcon's face. Then Falcon squeezed his trigger and Temela was blasted backwards. The big Zulu died on his feet, his chest smashed to a pulp. He was dead, and Falcon was up and running again before the shining bald head struck the ground.

Falcon shot down two more of Temela's men, and then his magazine was empty. Still he raced for the control centre. The East German guards who had taken cover inside threw open the door to receive him. He needed a few more seconds to get inside, but the back-up squads of terrorists were already rushing in from the perimeter fence.

Bullets chased him, and then a grenade was hurled to within a few feet of the doorway. It detonated with a crack of flame and the blast hurled Falcon off his feet. He hit the ground concussed and bleeding from the nose and mouth.

The stunned defenders inside the launch control centre backed off. They tried to escape through a rear exit and all three were cut down by another of the terrorist mop-up squads as they ran for the bush.

They were the last pocket of resistance. The battle was over.

Fifty per cent of Project *Vulcan* was now in flames, but there was one more fireball spectacular to finish off the night of death and destruction. The two MiG-17s had circled the launch site while Kitaka and his *Black K* forces had poured through the breached fences. They waited until the stuttering of small arms fire had ceased, and then came in to land.

The first MiG touched down safely on the runway, but the other attempted a triumphant flyover and a victory waggle of his wings. Unfortunately the pilot was not quite as skillful as he believed himself to be. Halfway through the manoeuvre he lost control, and the victory wriggle became a spiralling downward loop that plunged him smack into the bush.

Scarlet flame and black smoke plumed up from the thunderclap of sound, and again a section of the night was brightly illuminated. Jonas Kitaka stared toward the scene with a look of vague surprise on his face, then he shrugged his shoulders.

He had no further use for the MiG, so he did not particularly care about what had happened to the machine or its pilot. They had served their purpose.

CHAPTER 15

With the first light of dawn the atomic warhead which Kitaka had hijacked in South Africa was brought out of the jungle. It had been transported in a crude harness slung between two bullocks, and the cruelly whipped animals both collapsed with exhaustion at their journey's end. One of them immediately expired, the other was killed with an axe later in the day, and both animals were butchered for their meat.

The task of removing the harmless telecommunications satellite from the nose cone of the rocket, and replacing it with the warhead, was begun without delay.

The horrified and bewildered Doctor Praeger was kicked and beaten until he agreed to begin the work, and he was supervised in turn by Salem Sharif.

The Libyan had stayed discreetly in the background until the facility had been taken, and then he had gone direct to the launch pad with the warhead. He had been careful to avoid any contact with the captive journalists and the handful of survivors from the *Vulcan* workforce, all of whom were now being held in the undamaged guest huts. As an additional precaution he was also wearing one of the close black hoods with eye slits and one other slightly larger opening for the mouth. It masked his face, and helped to conceal the lighter colour of his skin. He had no intention of being seen without it until the final stage of *Firestrike* was complete.

In the meantime the only man other than the terrorists who would have any knowledge of his presence here would be Praeger. That could not be helped. It was necessary for him to work with Praeger. But afterwards Kitaka had assured him that the scientist would die. No matter what Praeger might learn or guess, the secret of the Libyan connection would be safe.

Kitaka held his own press conference later in the morning. His men marshalled the reluctant journalists inside the circle of guest huts, where Kitaka paraded before them in full *Black K* combat uniform with commander's epaulettes on his shoulders. Behind him the main block of administration buildings were blackened concrete shells, and the smell of blood and burning still lingered on the dry, dusty breeze.

Falcon was back among the press corps. He had recovered consciousness on his bed in the rondavel to find Helen gently bathing his face. She had told him that the terrorists had gathered up all the casualties, taking care of their own and dumping the rest in an empty guest hut. She had rescued him from there.

The sun was hot, blazing high overhead, and Falcon was still weak and dizzy. His head ached, but his iron will and constitution were helping him to make a slow recovery. He needed more rest, but he had to know what Kitaka intended.

While they waited for Kitaka to begin, Falcon looked carefully around the enclosure. He saw Hauptmann among the prisoners. The project director had a bloody dressing on his shoulder and his arm was supported with a sling, but at least he was still alive. Only an ashen-faced Doctor Olenga and a few of the senior technicians had survived with him.

A quick headcount of the armed terrorists who formed an outer circle round the prisoners gave a total of sixty-five. But Falcon knew there must be more. Kitaka would have men posted at the launch pad at least.

Kitaka began his speech, an arrogant, boastful tirade proclaiming his achievement this far. His audience listened in stony silence, and interest only flickered when he got to the point of introducing the slim young African in a pilot's flying suit who eventually joined him.

'This is our good friend Lieutenant Nereo, who has decided to leave the Mozambique Air Force and join our cause. The brave lieutenant, and his equally brave comrade who died, have both become disillusioned and disgusted with the Maputo government. They are ideologically committed to black rule for all of Africa, which the Maputo government has betrayed by its continued economic links with the white apartheid government in Pretoria. After today Lieutenant Nereo will not be able to return to Maputo, but he will be forever a hero of the black revolution.'

It was an extravagant introduction for a renegade who had deserted his country, but Nereo smiled and made a graceful bow to the press.

It was too much for the official representative of the Mozambique government. The distraught Doctor Olenga pushed forward and cried hysterically:

'He is a criminal! A traitor! A murderer!'

The butt of an AK-47 knocked him face down in the dust before he could say any more, but no one could doubt that his distress was genuine. To Olenga at least the actions of Lieutenant Nereo and his fellow pilot were a totally unexpected betrayal.

Kitaka ignored the interruption and continued with his speech. He had no more to say about the lieutenant anyway, for he intended only one name to be remembered and admired. That name, which he was determined would be bathed in glory, was Jonas Kitaka.

'You are wondering why we have done this.' He made a grand sweep of his arm to indicate the smouldering ruins on all sides. 'Now I will tell you. Two weeks ago the *Black K Liberation Army* attacked a South African military base and removed an atomic bomb. That was the first stage of operation *Firestrike*. The second stage was the capture of this rocket launching facility. The third and final stage will take place tomorrow, when we will launch the rocket, and the bomb, back into South Africa.'

He beamed proudly, and for a moment there was a total, disbelieving silence.

'You cannot,' Hauptmann said at last, although his face was white with fear. '*Vulcan One* cannot be adapted to carry a warhead.'

Kitaka scowled at him. 'Your good friend Doctor Praeger is working on it now. The task will be done, because the good doctor has been told that his life depends upon it.'

'We've heard nothing about an atomic bomb being stolen,' one of the reporters objected doubtfully.

'Of course not,' Kitaka sneered. 'The Pretoria government will not even admit that it has made the bomb. But the Pretoria government has committed this crime, and it is the criminals themselves who will see the crime explode in their faces.'

He laughed loudly and hilariously. 'It will be poetic justice — the first atomic warhead to explode in Africa will be their own bomb aimed against them.'

The journalists were exchanging anxious glances. The Frenchman bit his lip and said thoughtfully. 'There was an attack on an air base. They blew up fuel dumps and vehicles. But there was no mention of an atomic bomb.'

'There is a bomb,' Kitaka shouted at him. 'I — Jonas Kitaka — stole the bomb from the South Africans. And now it is here. It is being installed on that rocket.' He flung out a hand and pointed a dramatic finger toward the launch pad.

'It is a splendid joke,' he told them cheerfully. 'Pretoria has developed the bomb. Pretoria has built the bomb. But now the bomb has been stolen and Pretoria desperately wants it back. So the black revolution will help the white apartheid government in Pretoria. We are going to send their bomb back to Pretoria — on the *Vulcan* rocket.'

His men applauded with loud cheers and hand-clapping, and Kitaka laughed until the tears ran down his black cheeks. 'It is a joke,' he repeated. 'A joke!'

'It is madness,' Hauptmann protested. 'Even if you can destroy Pretoria you will kill many thousands of black Africans as well as white. You will kill *more* blacks than whites. You will incinerate your own people!'

'The white people have a saying,' Kitaka retorted. 'You cannot make omelettes without breaking eggs. The Bantu who will die in Pretoria will be expendable to our cause. It will be their own fault for being there and working for the white man.'

Hauptmann continued to argue, and several of the press men tried to support him, but Kitaka merely shouted them down. When the noise and the protests threatened to get out of hand the rank and file of terrorists moved in and knocked Hauptmann and two others to the ground. The angry silence returned while Kitaka raved on.

Falcon could recognize the futility of resistance at this stage, and he made no attempt to join the verbal opposition. Instead he watched Hauptmann's anguish and the reactions of his fellow journalists, and had to concede inwardly that the entire concept of what Kitaka had described as *Firestrike* had been very cleverly planned.

It had been convincingly demonstrated that none of the *Vulcan* directors on site, nor the weeping representative of the Mozambique government, had had any foreknowledge of what was going to happen. Also Falcon had so far seen no way in which Moscow or any of its communist allies could be linked to the impending rocket strike on Pretoria.

This far twenty of the world's most influential journalists had been swayed to a false belief by the evidence presented before their eyes. Except for Falcon himself, and perhaps Helen Collier, they were all ready to testify that South Africa, Mozambique and the East Germans, were all victims of a plot engineered by Kitaka and his terrorists, with no outside help other than that provided by the two renegade black pilots.

It was all happening exactly as Harry Killian had anticipated.

On the upper platform of the maintenance tower, a hundred feet above ground level, Praeger and Sharif had paused in their task of removing the satellite from the nose cone. They could hear Kitaka's speech being relayed over the tannoy speaker beside them and straightened their backs to listen.

Praeger's face was bruised, one lens of his spectacles was cracked and there were blood spots from a cut lip on the front of his white coat. He already knew what was happening, but the tone of the broadcast made him sweat and tremble.

He stared at the hooded man beside him. This one was cold and silent, different from the others. If he was African he was more Arabic than Bantu. A Palestinian perhaps, Praeger thought, but at least he had some technical knowledge. He was not ignorant. Perhaps he could be persuaded to see reason.

Praeger tried, pleading, arguing, almost choking over his own anguish.

'Shut up,' Sharif told him curtly.

'But the whole idea is monstrous. You are a man of some intelligence. You must see that your friend Kitaka is criminally insane. You cannot allow this holocaust to take place.'

'Shut up,' Sharif snarled at him. 'There is work to do. Get on with it.'

'I will not.' Praeger backed away until a rifle muzzle held by one of Kitaka's guards jabbed him mercilessly in the kidneys.

He gasped for breath, then found his voice again. 'It is impossible anyway. This rocket is not designed to hit a ground target.'

'We have discussed all this,' Sharif said wearily. 'The rocket has a guidance system. We will reduce the fuel load so it cannot reach orbit, and then it can be guided to target as it descends. I know about these things — enough to ensure that you will do what is required. Do not forget this!'

Praeger remained stubborn, until another jab of the rifle sent him staggering forward. Sharif caught him, held him almost gently for a moment, and then led him back to the nose cone. Praeger stood biting his lip until the blood trickled down his chin, and then slowly he resumed work.

Sharif watched him with impassive eyes, but inside he was not comfortable. The Libyan was being plagued more and more by his own inner doubts.

Kitaka had reached the end of his chest-thumping monologue, and he concluded with a warning. He held up a small radio transmitter and waved it in front of them.

'This was found in one of your guest huts. It means that one of you is a spy, but it does not matter.' He smiled to show his supreme confidence and contempt. 'I do not care which one of you is the spy, because now there is nothing any of you can do to stop me.'

He dropped the radio and stamped on it with the heel of his boot. There was a splintering sound as he crushed it into the dirt.

'Now there is no more spy radio. Remember also that the launch control centre, and the aircraft which brought you here, are both under heavy guard. There is no way that any of you can hope to escape from this place, or to send a message to the outside world.'

He grinned again at his captive audience, his black-bearded face split wide with enjoyment as he surveyed their shocked and anxious faces. At this moment he was the undisputed King Of The Heap, and he knew it.

'But do not be alarmed.' He threw them a crumb of comfort. 'You will all be allowed to leave here soon enough. The launching of the rocket, which you all came to observe, will be delayed by another twenty-four hours. That will give us time to change the payload, and to make adjustments to the guidance programme.

'But tomorrow at this time, the *Vulcan* rocket will be launched. You will all be witnesses. And afterwards we will permit you to go back on board your jet plane and return to Salisbury. You will all have a story for your newspapers — a better story than you bargained for. You will tell the world the name of Jonas Kitaka. *You will tell the world of My Victory!*'

CHAPTER 16

'That was your radio,' Falcon challenged Helen when they were alone again in the rondavel.

She had flopped out on the bed, grim-faced and thoughtful, and it was a moment before the words registered and she turned her head to face him. She hesitated, but her cover was unimportant now and she found she was glad to confess. She nodded.

'Yes, Mark. How long have you known?'

'That you were a BOSS agent? I suspected when Weissner released us after Soweto. I was certain when he let us go again to come here into Mozambique.'

Helen sat up, trying to read his face, relieved to see he wasn't angry. 'I was watching Kyller in the bar,' she admitted. 'Weissner wanted me to pick him up — try the old Mata Hari routine. But it wouldn't have worked. He wasn't my type, and he was already hooked with Judy Luys.'

'But I was your type?'

'Mark!' She was hurt and bit her lip. 'Mark, you were different. We struck sparks! I would have jumped into bed with you anyway, just for the sheer fun of it. We were there before Weissner ever knew you were in Johannesburg.'

'It's okay.' Falcon sat beside her and squeezed her hand. 'We're both grown up. And I have no complaints.'

She stared at him, then smiled faintly. Falcon tilted her chin up and kissed her gently on the lips. He let the kiss linger for a moment, and then became serious again.

'Weissner must have had some idea of what might happen. He'll have some kind of emergency plan. What is it?'

'A squadron of Mirage strike fighters on permanent standby at Hoedspruit. They're fully armed with air-to-ground missiles and ready for immediate scramble.' She blurted out the last of her secrets and with it her own personal anguish. 'But I was part of that plan, Mark. Weissner cannot order the jets to destroy Project *Vulcan* until he has cast-iron evidence that it has been taken over by terrorists. It was my job to send that warning, but without the radio there is no way.'

'So you didn't succeed in getting a message out?'

'No.' She bit her lip again with frustration. 'I tried, while you were trying to reach the control centre. But there was just too much bloody static breaking up my signal. The transmitter they gave me was small enough to keep hidden — but it wasn't powerful enough to do the bloody job.'

'Are you sure you didn't get through? That antenna on top of BOSS HQ in Pretoria looked big enough to pick up signals from Jupiter.'

'I know I failed. There should have been a codeword response, but when I switched to receive there was nothing but static. There must have been a sharp electrical storm somewhere between here and Pretoria.'

Falcon frowned and said nothing. He was thinking that she was probably right, for if the message had got through then by now they would have received a visit from the South African Air Force.

'I only had a few minutes,' Helen finished bitterly. 'Then I heard Kitaka's men hauling the other journalists out of their huts. I had to hide the radio quickly, but I didn't hide it well enough.'

'Perhaps we're fortunate Kitaka is so cocksure of himself,' Falcon said wryly. 'After our combined efforts last night a commander who was efficient as well as ruthless would have had both of us locked up. Instead we're free to try again.'

'But how?' Helen asked without hope in her voice. 'The control centre and the press corps jet are both being closely watched. The MiG-17 is still on the runway. There must be another radio there, but that will be guarded too. Kitaka knows a radio is our only hope of getting a message out.'

'I wasn't thinking of trying again for a radio. I was thinking of the other alternative.'

'What alternative?'

'To sabotage the rocket.'

Helen thought about it, then said slowly, 'Maybe. I don't see how, but if you can come up with a plan, then I think we could get some help. The scribbler's circus isn't entirely cowed. Most of those guys know you and some of them are looking to you for a lead. They know what you did last night, or at least some of it. The Frenchman and the American helped me carry you in here after I rescued you from the casualty heap.'

'No.' Falcon said firmly. 'This isn't a job for amateur volunteers.' He paused, searching for the right words, and finished softly, 'It isn't a job for a lady spy either.'

'Who said I was a lady?'

'I say you're a lady.' He smiled at her. 'What I'm really saying is that this job has to be a solo effort. We can't raise enough brute force to match Kitaka, so I have to play the invisible man.'

It was Helen's turn to frown. She said doubtfully, 'So what does the invisible man hope to do?'

'Get to Praeger,' Falcon answered simply. 'He's the key now, he's the only one who can reprogramme and control the launch.'

It made sense. Helen didn't want to be left behind, but she nodded agreement.

Falcon had to wait for darkness to make his move, which gave him more time to rest and recover his strength. There was plenty of time for thinking too, but he tried to avoid it. Praeger had all the essential technical knowledge, so until he could secure Praeger's help and advice it was impossible to make any detailed plan.

It was a long, sweltering hot day, but at last it came to an end. The spectacular African sunset was a panorama of flushed scarlet, radiating from a huge blood-red eyeball which slowly blinked its way below the horizon. The shadows thickened swiftly and night insects began to whir in the bush.

Falcon was again wearing dark clothing; a black sweatshirt with black slacks and black rubber-soled shoes. If he needed a weapon he would use his hands, for at this stage the only alternative to stealth and silence would be failure.

He had watched the movements of the terrorist guards patrolling the guest huts, and found them helpfully predictable. The guards strolled unconcerned around the outside of the circle of huts, their AK-47s slung casually over one shoulder. They were in no hurry and the circuit usually took five minutes, longer if they stopped to smoke or gossip, never less.

In fact, it was not the terrorists on official guard duty who provided a problem. The real risk came from the sheer number of terrorists wandering idly around the facility.

Falcon waited until the two duty guards had passed on their patrol and then slipped out of the rondavel window. He flattened himself upon the grass and began to wriggle slowly away from the hut. He had a hundred yards of open ground to cross to reach the executive bungalows, but there was no moon and the stars were not yet at their brightest.

It took him five minutes and twice he had to freeze against the stunted grass as the chatter of Bantu voices drifted near. No one stumbled over him and at last he reached the shadow of the low wall around the nearest bungalow. It was the same spot where he had paused the previous night before making his ill-fated effort to reach the control centre.

Three of the four executive bungalows were now occupied by Kitaka and his squad commanders. Koslowski was dead and Hauptmann and Olenga had both been bundled into the guest huts with the journalists. Only Praeger was kept apart and still permitted to sleep under his own roof.

Helen had kept watch while Falcon rested and had reported that Praeger had been brought back to the bungalow just before sunset. His bungalow was the third in the short row, which meant that Falcon had to crawl past two bungalows filled with terrorists to reach it.

He could hear loud laughter and the crash of discarded bottles. Light flooded through the open windows and when he briefly raised his head he saw half a dozen Africans playing cards in the nearest room. He put his head down and moved slowly along the garden wall.

He had to make a fast wriggle to pass each of the first two gateways, and once he had to lie perfectly still when a man wandered out onto one of the tiny lawns to urinate in a flower bed. The African returned to the party inside the bungalow and Falcon slowly exhaled and moved on.

Praeger's bungalow was in darkness, although with all the noise going on the scientist would have to be exhausted before he could sleep. There was no sign of a guard, but with the buildings on either side crowded with terrorists Kitaka had probably decided that a guard detail was unnecessary.

Falcon was duly grateful, for Kitaka's overconfidence was now the only real ace in his hand.

Falcon waited for a few moments, watching and listening, but the biggest danger of discovery now lay in delay. He drew a deep breath, eased up into a crouch, and then leaped swiftly over the garden wall to run fast and low for the open window of the bungalow. He was inside within seconds, freezing into silent stillness again, but there was no shout of alarm from outside.

He waited for his eyes to adjust to the greater darkness. A minute passed and outlines took shape in the gloom; an armchair, a writing desk, and bookshelves on the wall. He was in a living room that was used as a study. He located the door and moved toward it. On the other side was a short hallway, and three more doors. He guessed kitchen, bathroom and bedroom.

He eased open what he hoped was the bedroom door. Starlight filtered through another open window directly opposite and he knew he was right. The silhouette of a man lay sprawled on the bed beneath the window.

The man stirred abruptly, twisting and reaching for the bedside lamp. It clicked on and light spilled over the head of the bed. The man was Praeger, blinking without his glasses.

'It's all right,' Falcon said quickly, and even as he spoke he realized it was not.

Praeger was not alone. There was an armchair in the corner of the room and a man sat there on guard. The man was hooded, his eyes alert and gleaming through narrow slits, and in one hand he held an automatic pistol aimed at Falcon's heart.

'Be still,' Salem Sharif commanded grimly. 'Otherwise I shall be obliged to kill you.'

CHAPTER 17

The pistol was a Russian Tokarev, but what was really interesting was the hand which held it.

Falcon realized in that moment that there *was* a link to one of the pro-Moscow satellite regimes, either Syria, Libya or Iraq. He also understood why so many of the terrorists had worn the seemingly unnecessary balaclava-type hoods. They were a device to hide the identity of just one man — the masked man who was now pointing the Tokarev at his stomach.

It was Praeger who spoke next, his voice thin and wavering. He had the haggard face of a man who had looked into hell, and he groped for his spectacles so that he could see more clearly.

'Who are you? What do you want?'

'My name is Falcon. I'm one of the journalists,' Falcon answered quietly.

Salem Sharif rose carefully to his feet. All his senses told him this man was dangerous, and he knew he was at a slight disadvantage while he remained seated. Something about Falcon was familiar, and the dark clothing gave him a clue. Last night he had watched this man in action from the edge of the bush.

'You are the one who tried to reach the control centre,' he accused quietly. 'You killed the big zulu, and most of his squad.'

Falcon turned to face him. Once the hooded man raised his voice to attract attention it would be the end, so there was nothing to lose, and just possibly something to be gained by keeping him talking. He let himself relax, trying to put the other man off guard, and nodded ruefully.

'I had a go. I'm afraid I didn't get very far.'

'You made a very good try,' Sharif complimented him. 'And tonight you are trying again. You are not just an ordinary journalist.'

'And you are no ordinary terrorist,' Falcon returned calmly. 'So who are you?'

'He is a technician of some kind.' Praeger spoke bitterly. 'He has watched over me while I have been forced to work. I have tried to make delays, to pretend that what they wanted was not possible, but I could not fool him. I do not think he could do the work himself, but he knows what can be done.'

'So the work is finished?'

'Yes.' Praeger lowered his head into his hands. 'May God have pity on me, but I have done what they asked. I have removed the satellite and installed the warhead. The rocket has been fuelled and is ready to be fired.'

'But you came here to stop it,' Sharif guessed shrewdly. 'Sabotage, that must be your plan. But you need Doctor Praeger's help, and you did not expect to find me here.'

'You are a surprise,' Falcon conceded wryly.

Sharif stared at him thoughtfully, then shifted his gaze to Praeger. 'And you, Doctor? If I had not been here — would you have helped him?'

Praeger looked up, surprised by the question. For a moment he was uncertain, and then he found a spark of courage and said firmly: 'Yes, I would have helped.'

'How?' The demand was curt and urgent.

Praeger had been wrestling all day with his conscience and he had the answer ready. 'I would rewire the warhead. It can be made to explode upon launching instead of upon impact. I could not do it while you were constantly looking over my shoulder, but it is possible.'

'Then you would kill everyone here at Project *Vulcan*.'

'Better that than a whole city.' Praeger glared at his hooded tormentor. 'Most of my friends here are dead anyway. And I shall be killed as soon as my work is finished. Your presence here is too vital a secret. Your friends will not let me live.'

'No,' Sharif said softly. 'And I do not believe that I am intended to live either.'

He lowered the Tokarev automatic and pulled off his mask. The decision had been a hard one to reach and his heart was heavy, but there was some relief as he threw the hood away.

'I am prepared to help you,' he volunteered, because this way he still had some choice in the way he would die.

They closed the shutters to ensure a greater degree of privacy, and then Salem Sharif explained his change of heart.

'In 1969 I was one of the group of young officers who brought about the coup which put Colonel Gaddafi into power in Libya,' he told them quietly. 'You must understand that then Gaddafi was a great man. We all shared the brilliance of his ambition and his dreams. We would all have given our lives for Gaddafi, for Arab Socialism, and for Libya.' He looked hard at Falcon. 'I am still a patriot. I would still give my life for Arab Socialism, and for Libya.'

'But not for Colonel Gaddafi,' Falcon suggested.

'Gaddafi has changed. His policies are too extreme. In the end they can only be harmful to Libya.' Sharif paused, thinking back, then continued, 'I was the youngest of the coup group, and since then I have become Gaddafi's envoy to terrorist groups throughout the world. I have undertaken missions to the Lebanon, to the Philippines, to Italy, Germany and

Northern Ireland. I have funnelled cash and arms to fanatics of all colours — to the PLO, the IRA, the Red Brigades and the others — and arranged for the most violent of their young men to be sent back to Libya for training in death and destruction.'

Praeger looked as though he wanted to interrupt, but Falcon motioned him to silence. A picture of gradual disillusionment was emerging, and he wanted Sharif to go on.

'I suppose the turning point for me was Uganda,' Sharif remembered with a grimace. 'I was one of the commanders of the Libyan parachute force which rescued Idi Amin from the Tanzanians. Gaddafi had always supported Amin, but what I saw in Amin's torture chambers turned my stomach. I came away sickened and I asked myself, why had it been necessary for Libya to support such a monster?'

Sharif sighed and shook his head, an indication of his inability to answer his own question. Then he defended his own heart-searching.

'Today there are many people in Libya who have the same doubts. The atrocities of Idi Amin have opened many eyes. In the bazaars and cafes of Tripoli and Benghazi there is a growing disenchantment with the policies of Colonel Gaddafi. The people have started to question the unrestricted use of Libya's oil wealth to support terrorists and dictators. For myself I began to realize that to blindly support Gaddafi may not be the best way to serve Libya.'

His English was good, but he needed another pause to select his words, then he continued: 'I have met with many terrorists. I still have sympathy with the Palestinians, for theirs is a just cause, but all the others are insane. And this Jonas Kitaka is the biggest madman of them — he is showing all the bloody potential of another Idi Amin!'

He turned to face Praeger. 'I made you work, Doctor, because I believed that Kitaka would give the South Africans an ultimatum. I believed he would ask for political equality for black men in South Africa — for an end to apartheid in return for the city of Pretoria. *But he has asked for nothing.* He is simply going to destroy Pretoria, and all the people in it.'

Sharif stood up and began to pace the room in his agitation. He pounded his fist into the palm of his hand.

'I will not be a part of this atrocity. I will not! I cannot see how the destruction of Pretoria can serve *my* country. I cannot see how the destruction of this city can serve any useful purpose. Let Allah be my judge — not Gaddafi — for I will not help to create another Idi Amin!'

He calmed himself to face Falcon again, and offered his hand. 'We will work together,' he repeated. 'I will help you to sabotage the rocket.'

Falcon left Praeger's bungalow in the same way he had arrived, silently, stealthily, and alone. He got well clear of the bungalows, making a wide circle around the launch control centre, and on the dirt road out to the launch pad he waited.

Five minutes passed before Sharif appeared with Praeger. The Libyan had simply donned his hood again and marched Praeger ahead of him. It was a cool gamble and he had a plausible story ready to meet any challenge, but no bluff was needed. Perhaps they had been seen, or perhaps they had not, but no voice had called out to question their departure.

'They are too busy with their beer and cards,' Sharif said with disgust for his former allies. 'They think their victory is already won.'

Falcon smiled. He was counting on it, but there was no time to waste. 'Let's go,' he said. 'Maybe we'll surprise them yet.'

It had been too risky to take a vehicle so they had half a mile to walk. The moon was now coming up through the clouds on the horizon, and there was more light than they wanted. However, it could not be helped. They moved as fast as Praeger could manage. The scientist was feeling his age, his breathing was laboured and he stumbled often, but he was as determined as any of them to see the job done.

The rocket rose before them like a magnet, a giant black spear into the jewelled vault of the night sky, with the latticed black maintenance tower still beside it. The hinged tower was not due to fold back until the final dawn checks had been made.

'There will be three guards,' Sharif told Falcon as they trotted towards it. 'Kitaka has posted strong guards wherever there is a radio, but he has not seriously considered that any of you will try to do anything more than pass a message or run away into the bush.'

Falcon calculated the problem and made his battle plan. He passed it back to Sharif who shrugged and nodded. The Libyan knew it was all going to be a balance of luck and bluff however they played it.

Sharif slowed to a walk to let Praeger get his breath back, and Falcon ran on ahead. When he was still two hundred yards short of the launch pad Falcon moved off the road and began to circle through the low scrub and clumps of thorn bush. He had to employ all his stealth and cunning again, darting swiftly from shadow to shadow as he moved in close. For the last fifty yards he was down on his belly again, as silent and as deadly as any carnivore predator that had ever stalked the savage face of Africa.

He pinpointed two of the guards. One of them was seated on the discarded sphere of the satellite, which had been dumped carelessly on the ground. The other was squatting in front of him. Both had their AK-47s slung on one shoulder. They were smoking and talking. Falcon looked for number three but failed to find him.

Cautiously he circled behind the launch pad, and then up on to the walled concrete slab itself to slip into deep shadow below the maintenance tower. Still there was no sign of the third guard and he looked upward, frowning and wondering. Then there was a sharp sound of exclamation from the man sitting on the satellite. Sharif and Praeger had appeared, walking calmly up the dirt road.

The two terrorists unslung their combat rifles and went warily forward. Praeger was clearly identified by his white coat, and Sharif by his hood, but their late return on foot was still cause for suspicion.

Sharif raised a hand casually in greeting. 'It is okay,' he told them. 'But we must go up to the nose cone again. There is something I must check.'

The guards relaxed a little, and began asking questions. They received no answers because by then Falcon had moved up silently behind them. The hard edge of his palm slashed down across an exposed neck and the first guard crumpled. The second African started to turn and Falcon kicked him hard and low in the stomach. As the man doubled in agony the Falcon's fist cracked up in a lightning uppercut to the jaw.

Sharif had started to move forward but he was not needed. Both guards were sprawled senseless on the dirt. Falcon stooped to pick up the fallen rifles and tossed one to the Libyan.

'You said there were three,' he said softly.

'There were three when we left.' Sharif looked worried and glanced up at the rocket and the tower.

'I'll check it out,' Falcon murmured.

He left Sharif and Praeger to drag the two unconscious terrorists off the road and into the scrub and swiftly ran back to the launch pad. The tower stretched above him in a vertical square tunnel of steel, criss-crossed by flights of steel stairways. He stared upward, looking for movement, and then slung the AK-47 over his right shoulder and began to climb.

At fifty feet he paused on one of the platforms, again searching the shadows above him. If the third guard was up there he was either asleep or uncertain. The top was still another fifty feet up, high enough for the guard to be confused about what might be happening on ground level.

Asleep? Alert and waiting for him to come up? Or not there at all?

Falcon did not know, but he could not afford to take chances. He stepped off the stairway and walked the steel tightrope of a girder to the corner of the tower, and there he continued his ascent on the outside.

His upward progress was slow, for it was a dangerously long stretch between the girders. There were times when he was hanging from the bolt heads by his fingers and toes, and there was nothing to check his fall if he had slipped. Also he did not dare to make a sound. Just one scratch or scrape could be fatal now, for if there was a guard he was hopelessly vulnerable.

Like a human fly he inched his way up the outside of the tower. The concrete launch pad was sixty feet below. Then Seventy. Eighty. And at eighty-five feet above ground level he froze.

The third guard was venturing slowly down the inside of the maintenance tower. His AK-47 was gripped tightly in his sweating hands, and he was pausing at every level to peer down into the gloom. He had been disturbed by the initial scuffle from below, and now his nerves had frayed with waiting.

Falcon clung to the corner of the tower and allowed the man to pass. Then he cat-walked back across to the stairway. The guard was below him and suddenly sensed his presence. The startled man whirled and looked up.

Falcon was on the stairway, both hands on the guard rails, his arms stiffened to take his weight as he slid down fast with both feet thrust forward. He had made himself into a human battering ram. His heels smashed into the African's chest and the guard was somersaulted backward into space. He screamed once on the way down and then there was total silence.

Falcon continued his climb to the top and waited there for Sharif and Praeger to join him. When they arrived the scientist needed a few moments to rest from his exertions, so it was Sharif who unscrewed the inspection panel and removed it from the nose cone of the *Vulcan* rocket.

Finally Praeger accepted the return of his screwdriver, and with Sharif holding a flashlight and Falcon standing guard he began his task of sabotage.

CHAPTER 18

It took just under forty minutes for Praeger to complete the rewiring of the warhead. He worked in silent concentration, and when at last he withdrew his head and shoulders from the nose cone his face was dripping with perspiration. He was white and hollow eyed, like a grey-haired zombie emerging from a Turkish bath. Very carefully he screwed the inspection panel back into place, and then he looked down at his hands.

They began to tremble. It was an involuntary reaction after the sustained strain and tension, and once the shaking had begun he could not stop it.

'It is finished,' he croaked hoarsely. 'When Kitaka presses the launch button the warhead will explode immediately. Pretoria is safe, but every human being within a mile radius of the launch pad will be roasted in the fireball.'

'I've been thinking about that,' Falcon said quietly. 'We'll have to try and do something to get the press corps and the *Vulcan* people away.'

'Warn them,' Sharif said. 'That is all we can do. Tell them to escape if they can, and run far into the bush.'

'They may not be able to run far enough. The flash fire from this thing could set half of Africa ablaze.'

Sharif looked at him uncertainly, and then a wry smile played at the corners of his mouth. 'You have been making plans again?'

Falcon nodded. His brain had been active while he had kept watch and Praeger had worked, and from this height he had been able to overlook the whole diamond pattern of roads linking the moon shadowed outposts of the launch site.

'Over there—' He pointed at the thin, just visible track of the dirt road leading to the storage area. 'The liquid fuel store for the rocket. Highly volatile stuff. If we can find some explosive and blow it up it should make quite a promising diversion.'

'They used gelignite to clear some areas of the site for construction,' Praeger offered doubtfully. 'I believe there is some left — and some time fuses.'

'What do we hope to achieve behind this diversion?' Sharif asked more practically.

'We are armed.' Falcon weighed the captured AK-47 in his hands to illustrate his meaning. 'If we can create enough confusion to draw the bulk of Kitaka's men away from the guest huts and the runway, then perhaps we can get the hostages to the press corps jet.'

'You ask for much.'

Falcon shrugged. 'We've got nothing better to do between now and sunrise. The air crew are being held with the press, so if we can recapture the plane and get them all on board, they can fly it to safety.'

Sharif smiled, his teeth gleaming white in the moonlight. He had done as his conscience dictated and now he no longer cared about what might happen next. Even if he survived he knew he could never return to Libya. In the meantime the idea appealed to him.

'We could also blow up the radar screens,' he suggested. 'And the storage sheds. I think Kitaka has only two guards on the fuel store. The rest he has no need for, so he has not bothered to guard it at all.' His smile widened. 'I think together we can make some pretty spectacular diversions.'

They still had three hours before dawn, but there was a lot of ground to be covered and so there was no time to waste. They climbed down from the maintenance tower and turned their backs on the launch pad to jog-trot over to the storage area. After the first quarter mile Praeger was again left to rest, while Falcon and Sharif continued ahead to scout the terrain.

They checked out the two huge radar screens, glinting like angled steel saucers as they caught the moonlight. There were no guards, which was a promising sign, and after a brief inspection they ran on.

There were three of the long storage buildings facing on to a hard tarmac loading area, and then the fuel store located a safe one-hundred and fifty yards further back All the buildings had padlocked doors at the front and back, but a careful reconnaissance showed that Sharif was again right about the guards. Kitaka had posted only two of his men to watch over the whole complex.

The two Africans were hard to find, but eventually the low murmur of their voices and the glow of a cigarette gave them away. They were seated on the ground with their backs propped against the gnarled trunk of a huge old baobab tree, some fifty feet away from the building they were supposed to protect. There were prominent NO SMOKING signs plastered all over the fuel store, which was why the guards were keeping their distance.

Both men were relaxed, talking just enough to keep themselves awake. The moon had passed behind another patchwork of passing cloud and the bush around them was full of familiar rustles and nocturnal movement. The night insects made their whirring music, and somewhere outside the perimeter fence a hunting cat made a brief grunting cough.

The guards stirred warily, remembering that the perimeter fence had been smashed open. Then they relaxed again because the lion or leopard was far away. In that moment a dry leaf was softly crunched behind them.

The two Africans started to rise in panic, their hearts thumping, their minds filled with the fear of charging lion or some other jungle predator. But it was Salem Sharif whose foot had crushed the leaf. He struck down once with the butt of his rifle and smashed the nearest African between the eyes. Falcon had whirled out from behind the other side of the baobab tree, and dropped the second guard with an identical blow.

Both guards were sprawled senseless. The scuffle had taken less than five seconds and the noise had been minimal. Falcon looked at Sharif and they both smiled. Each knew that in the other he had found a useful ally.

'I will fetch Praeger,' Sharif offered.

Falcon nodded and Sharif hurried back the way they had come. Falcon paused to make a closer check of the two unconscious Africans, collecting up their combat rifles, and thoughtfully taking charge of two Russian-made hand grenades he found clipped to one man's belt. The night was still young and he had the feeling they might come in useful.

He moved over to the fuel store and removed the padlock. He used the barrel of one of the spare rifles, inserting it through the steel hasp and then twisting viciously until he had snapped the lock open. Moving back to the main storage buildings he quickly dealt with the padlocks there.

He was searching the general store where the maintenance tools and spare parts were kept when Sharif returned with Praeger. He had not found what he wanted but the scientist led them straight to the far end of the building and pointed out four wooden boxes filled with six-ounce sticks of gelignite.

'There are detonators here,' Sharif added cheerfully, lifting down a smaller cardboard box from an upper shelf. Inside there were half a dozen of the little metal tubes, each one about half the size of a ballpoint pen.

'And the fuses.' Praeger pulled forward another box.

Falcon checked them over. 'The detonators are okay,' he told them. 'But not the fuses. These are only a sixty-second delay. Good enough for blasting out tree stumps, but we want to be well clear on the other side of the launch site when our fireworks start to go off.'

Praeger looked uncertain, but Falcon was slipping off his wristwatch. Sharif flashed an understanding smile and did the same.

'Yours too, Doctor. With these I can rig up a sixty-minute delay.' Praeger surrendered his wristwatch.

'I shall need some flashlight batteries,' Falcon continued. 'There should be some of those about. And the loan of your screwdriver and pliers.'

Praeger handed over the tools he had used to rewire the warhead and went in search of the batteries.

'One of the guards we knocked out had a wristwatch,' Sharif recalled. 'I will fetch it. That will give us four.'

Falcon nodded approval and Sharif went out. There were spools of electrical wire on the shelf beside the detonators and Falcon carried everything he needed to a workbench where he risked switching on a light. He cut the plastic-coated wire into the required lengths and began the intricate task of assembling the first bomb.

Praeger returned with a box of flashlight batteries and watched doubtfully as Falcon worked. He had the technological knowledge to deal with the advanced warhead, but on this crude level, playing with sweating gelignite, he was distinctly alarmed.

'Are you sure you know what you are doing?' he asked anxiously.

Falcon paused to reassure him. 'I had extensive military training, Doctor. They taught me everything there is to know about sabotage with conventional explosives, including how to construct or dismantle terrorist bombs.'

Praeger shuddered. 'If you don't mind,' he said politely. 'I will wait outside.'

When the bombs were finished there was still about an hour and thirty minutes of darkness left before the dawn. Falcon set each of the wristwatch timers for the maximum delay — the minute hands would have to make a complete sweep before touching the hour hands to trigger the circuit — and then the bombs were placed in position.

One was strapped to the cylindrical five-thousand-gallon fuel propellant tank inside the fuel store.

Two and three were placed inside the radar tracking stations beneath each of the two huge disc screens.

The final time bomb served for all three of the storage buildings. Sharif had linked them together with rivers of spilled petrol from conventional fuel drums. The spare gelignite he had split into two piles in the second and third buildings and he had calmly poured more petrol on top. It was an operation which Praeger had watched with nail-biting horror.

When it was done they hurried back toward the main administration complex and the guest huts. They moved more cautiously as they approached over the last few hundred yards, for Kitaka still had more than eighty of his heavily armed terrorists in the area. Falcon stopped while they were still in cover of the bush and made Praeger take off his white coat and throw it away. Underneath he wore dark trousers and a grey shirt which would be less noticeable.

It was here that Sharif decided to leave them.

'Most of the Africans will run toward the explosions to see what is happening,' he told Falcon calmly. 'But some of their squad commanders are not complete fools. Kitaka especially has great animal cunning, and enough military experience to recognize a diversion. I will have to do something extra to lead him away if you are to succeed in getting your friends to the plane.'

Falcon was surprised, but there was no time for questions and explanations. The time bombs were ticking off the seconds and as abruptly as he had made his decision the Libyan turned and disappeared into the night.

Praeger looked startled and uncertain, but Falcon knew instinctively that they could still trust the man who had helped them this far. He urged Praeger on and they continued toward the guest huts.

Helen had been watching and waiting beside the window, trapped in a prolonged agony of suspense until at last she had dozed on her feet. She came awake with a start as Falcon and Praeger slipped in through the door behind her, turning and almost falling as she tried to move her stiffened limbs. Falcon caught her neatly in his arms.

'Mark!' she blurted in anguish. 'You've been gone for hours. I've been scared sick. What on earth have you been doing?'

Falcon sat down on the bed and told her, explaining everything as quickly as he could without omitting any detail. Her eyes widened as she took it all in and he felt a tremor run through her body.

'Bloody hell,' she said at last. 'What happens next?'

'I've brought you one of these.' Falcon handed her one of the spare AK-47s he had collected during his travels. 'There are two more you can hand out once you get the circus together. I know there's at least a couple of those press guys who will want to volunteer.'

'I've got to get them together?'

Falcon nodded. 'I'm sorry, BOSS lady, but I'm going to be too busy. I'll take you and Doctor Praeger over to the hut on the far side of the circle — the one nearest the runway. There I'll have to leave him with you, and you'll have to get the rest of the press corps assembled. When the balloon goes up wait a minute to give Kitaka's boys time to start running in the wrong direction, then break out and lead the circus at full speed up the runway.'

'As easy as that,' she said gloomily.

'It won't be easy,' Falcon admitted. 'Maybe they won't all make it, but it's the best chance we can give them.' He smiled at her and squeezed her hand. 'Helen, I wouldn't ask you if I didn't know you were brave enough to do it.'

'Thanks, Mark.' She gave him an impulsive kiss. 'But what about you? If you're leaving all this to me, then you must be planning something even more dangerous?'

'I'm going ahead to secure the plane,' he told her. 'I was hoping to have Sharif's help, but he's got something else in mind. Anyway, I can do it alone. As soon as I can I'll double back to meet you and give you covering fire.'

Helen pulled her face into a grimace. 'Mark, this is going to be bloody.'

'I know.' Falcon shrugged helplessly. 'But at least this time the surprise factor will be on our side.'

CHAPTER 19

The fuel store blew up just as the first pale pink cracks of dawn began to spread up from the eastern horizon. There was a deafening crack of thunderous sound, and the flameburst boiled and roared like a minor Hiroshima. On the opposite side of the launch site there were only two windows in the whole administration complex which had survived the original air attack, and they both shattered from the blast.

The radar stations exploded ten and fifteen seconds later. The control rooms which formed the base for each screen virtually disintegrated and collapsed, and the huge, circular webs of steel toppled forward to crash down in the bush.

The chain reaction of destruction continued as the first storage building erupted. A thin river of fire flashed across the intervening open ground to the petrol-soaked piles of gelignite in buildings two and three, and they were ripped apart by successive fire blasts to add to the general holocaust.

The tinder-dry bush ignited to link up the separate explosions and within less than a minute the entire north point perimeter of the *Vulcan* launch site had the appearance of an advancing tidal wave of towering flames.

Kitaka had posted six of his men to guard the press corps jet. Two of them were sitting on the bottom step of the gangway which was still in position at the open door, and the other four were fast asleep in the reclining seats in the passenger cabin.

The first supersonic boom shook them all awake. The two men on the gangway lurched to their feet, grabbing for their combat rifles, but then staring with blank, open-mouthed amazement down the runway. The four men inside the plane struggled to get out, the man at the rear pushing his companions further down the steps so that he too could see what was happening.

Falcon had spent half an hour circling through the bush to get into position, and now he was crouched between the shoulder-high landing wheels of the aircraft. He waited another thirty seconds, just in case there were more stragglers to come out of the plane. Then he moved out under the black shadow of the wing, his AK-47 at the ready.

The six Africans were bunched up on the gangway, shouting with excitement and with all their attention fixed on the fiery spectacular of the skyline. One of them turned to say something to his companions, and saw the movement of that darker shadow of death beneath the wing.

With six of them and with so much at stake Falcon could not afford to take chances. He triggered the AK-47 and scythed the burst of bullets at chest height up the line of the gangway. The guards spun and fell and tumbled down into an untidy, crimson-splattered heap on the runway.

The Falcon was already moving, running forward, vaulting over the still-quivering tangle of limbs, and bounding up the gangway three steps at a time. He dived low through the doorway, crouching into immediate cover between two of the seats with the AK-47 again at the ready. It was all unnecessary because the aircraft was empty.

He made a fast check, forward on to the flight deck, and then doubling back down the full length of the passenger cabin to be sure. When he was satisfied he left the plane. He paused only to double-check the dead guards, and to rob two of the bodies of spare magazines for his rifle, and then he was racing at full speed back down the centre of the runway.

Helen had succeeded in getting the majority of the hostages into the one hut. It had been a nerve-wracking business, waiting for the guards to pass, then wriggling over to each rondavel in turn, waking the occupants and bringing them back before the guards could complete their circuit. Fortunately the guards were slack and sleepy, more clouds had rolled up to obscure the moon and increase the cover of darkness, and the journalists were all level-headed and capable men who had had their nerves tested on previous danger-area assignments.

She had cleared every hut and when she had completed the circle only three faces were missing. The hut Hauptmann had shared with two of his senior technicians had been empty. Kitaka had sent for them early in the evening, and they had been taken over to the launch control centre to work all night on the revised calculations for the dawn countdown.

There was nothing Helen could do to help them. She could only concentrate on those she had been able to get together, briefing them on what to expect, detailing the able-bodied in pairs to help the wounded, and issuing the spare rifles to the American and the Frenchman.

When the explosions finally rocked the entire launch site there was pandemonium among Kitaka's men. Some of them ran toward the wall of leaping flames. Others ran away from it. There arose the mistaken belief that they had been hit by a South African air strike, and many of them began to run for the safety of the bush.

Helen gave them half a minute as Falcon had advised. Time to be totally distracted by the shock, but not time to recover from it. Then she gave the terse order to move.

The scribbler's circus, and the oddments of *Vulcan* personnel, left the rondavel at a run. Helen and her rearguard were out first, moving left and right to deal with any interference, and letting the mainstream pass between them before they followed behind. She had chosen her moment well and they got almost to the runway before they were spotted. The two terrorists who had been patrolling the guest huts realized what was happening and shouted in alarm. They began an immediate pursuit, but Helen dropped on to one knee to wait for them, and then cut them down with her AK-47 as they ran toward her.

She sprang up again, wheeling and racing to catch up with her charges as they reached the beginning of the runway. There was more pursuit from behind and hot bursts of automatic fire chased after them. Helen realized that they were too exposed on the open concrete and yelled at them to take cover in the bush.

The fugitives veered off the runway and into the tangled clumps of thorn and scrub. They had to zigzag now as they tried to keep moving parallel to the runway and their progress was slowed. Behind them a score of terrorists were coming up fast, and Helen and her two armed companions threw themselves flat on the edge of the runway and tried desperately to hold the enemy back.

Falcon saw what was happening: the circus scattered in the bush, and the terrorists trying to take the direct route down the runway to head off their escaping prisoners before they could reach the jet plane. It wasn't working out at all as well as he had hoped, and he had to do something fast.

He was already halfway down the half-mile length of the runway, racing at full speed and still too far away to effectively intervene. And even when he got there he would only add one more rifle to the rearguard.

He needed more firepower, and he saw a possible answer looming out of the darkness on his right. It was the parked MiG-17 that had been hijacked from the Mozambique Air Force.

Falcon changed direction and sprinted toward it. He was only twenty yards away when a man suddenly stood up from beneath the wing, pointed a revolver at him and fired.

Falcon recognized the slim figure in the flying suit. The man was Lieutenant Nereo. For some reason, perhaps in anticipation of a possible attack by the South African Air Force, the renegade pilot had decided to sleep by his machine.

Falcon swerved as the gun banged. He saw the flash of muzzle flame and felt the hot burn of the bullet as it ripped through his sleeve and just grazed his upper arm. Then he fired the AK-47 and Nereo was cut down and his body hammered under the fuselage out of the way.

Falcon leaped up onto the wing, slid back the sliding canopy and dropped down into the pilot's seat. It took him a minute to explore the unfamiliar controls and then he switched on the instrument panel light. A glance over the dials showed that the fuel tanks were almost empty. However, he did not intend to fly the machine, but simply to get it moving at ground level. He started the engine, reached down for the throttle control on his right-hand side, and began to taxi forward.

The MiG gathered speed, and Falcon used it as a tank to charge down the centre of the runway. He had noted that the wing hardpoint racks were empty — Nereo had used up all the rockets — but he was hoping there might be a few shells left for the cannon.

He lined up the optical gunsight at eye level in front of him with the main bunch of terrorists charging on to the runway. Then he thumbed down the red firing button. The 23-

millimetre cannon under the right side of the nose was empty, but there were two on the left and one of those was still loaded. There was a comforting hammer of fire, and Falcon zigzagged the skidding MiG to spread the devastating pattern of shell bursts across the full width of the runway.

As Jonas Kitaka emerged from the bungalow he had commandeered as his HQ he was temporarily stunned by the chaos exploding on all sides. A gigantic thick black smoke cloud blanketed the sky to the north and beneath it the sea of red fire was visibly expanding in waves of thirty-foot flames. His men were scattering in all directions and in the next few minutes he shouted himself hoarse as he chased after his squad commanders and brought them to order.

The crackle of rifle fire from the direction of the runway alerted him to the fact that his hostages were escaping. For a moment he was torn by indecision, but then his extensive military training and the long years of experience stretching back through time and place to the Congo helped him to put the salient points into perspective.

There had been no roar of jet fighters overhead, so this was not an air attack. Therefore it had to be a ground attack from outside, or sabotage from within. Either way the explosions were coming from the lightly-guarded and non-vital corner of the facility. They were a diversion, and the strategy was succeeding.

Controlled fury gave Kitaka the strength and power to restore his chain of command. He rallied his own squad and then bawled at his other squad leaders to get their teams together. One group he despatched to double the guard at the control centre, and another he sent running out to check the launch pad.

Next he turned his attention to the escaping journalists. Some of his men were already in pursuit and he yelled at the rest to follow him and give them support. He no longer cared about witnesses to observe his triumph, only that his moment of glory should not be taken away.

'Kill them!' he screamed with all the power of his lungs. 'Destroy their aeroplane! Do not let any of them escape!'

About forty of the *Black K* guerrillas were urged forward by his call, hurrying to reinforce those who were already engaged in battle with Helen and her rearguard. Those odds would have been impossible, but in that moment the MiG-17 roared up out of the night, hurling the last of its canon shells down the runway.

Kitaka and the bulk of his force were moving up through the guest huts when the shells slaughtered the vanguard and exploded all around them. Three of the thatch-roofed rondavels burst into flame and again the terrorist army scattered in confusion.

Kitaka howled at them to regroup, but then a strong hand on his shoulder spun him round. He found himself staring face to face with Salem Sharif.

'Let them go, Jonas!' the Libyan said urgently. 'The important thing is to fire the rocket before it is too late!'

Kitaka gaped at him, trembling with rage and for the moment speechless. The only thought in his mind was to kill the hostages and all his instincts were primed to storm the runway. He tried to wrench his arm away, but with a surprising display of strength Sharif held him back.

'The rocket!' Sharif repeated desperately. 'As soon as one of them gets to the plane they will use the radio. Perhaps they have already done so. The South African Air Force could be on its way now with air-to-ground missiles. We must act now.

Withdraw all our forces to the control centre, hold it — and launch the rocket while there is still time.'

Kitaka faltered, but slowly the logic of the argument began to override his dominant fury. He realized the Libyan could be right. There could be a squadron of Mirage strike fighters speeding toward them. Panic filled him, because he could not bear to see *Firestrike* fail. He spun on his heel, screamed at his men to follow, and with Sharif running beside him he led the way back to the control centre.

The MiG-17 had fired its last shell. The guns were empty and Falcon braked his improvised tank to a stop. The circus was behind him now. Helen had hustled the journalists back onto the runway and they were running with a clear start toward the press corps jet at the far end.

Falcon stood up in the cockpit and emptied the magazine of his AK-47 toward the last of the retreating terrorists who had broken and fled before the MiG's attack. Then he jumped down to the runway and backed off.

As a final gesture he unclipped one of the hand grenades from his belt, pulled the pin, and tossed it into the open cockpit. The MiG blew up in another satisfying fireball.

Falcon raced back up the runway, fitting a fresh magazine to the AK 47 as he went.

Hauptmann and his two senior technicians had been standing at the toughened observation window in the control centre, staring in horror at the flames and carnage outside. Their hearts were beating fast and they recoiled with alarm when the door burst open and Kitaka, Sharif, and a dozen of the terrorists surged inside.

'Begin the launch,' Kitaka ordered harshly. 'Fire now! There is no time to waste.'

'It is impossible,' Hauptmann protested. 'There is a correct procedure to be followed.'

'Do not play games with me!' Kitaka roared with rage and smashed his combat rifle into Hauptmann's face. As the site director fell unconscious he whirled ferociously on the nearest technician. 'Where is the firing button. Tell me!'

'Here.' The sweating scientist pointed out the red button on the control panel. 'But Herr Hauptmann told you the truth. We have to go through the countdown and pre-ignition sequence. And the maintenance tower is still in position.'

'Then begin,' Kitaka snarled. 'Get the tower down. And do not waste time with any unnecessary checks. I give you five minutes — and if the rocket has not been launched I will kill all of you.'

It was no idle threat and they knew it. The two technicians were white-faced with terror and they hurried to obey.

A television screen came alive to show *Vulcan One* standing proud and erect on its launch pad. Behind it, giving the nose cone an unholy red halo, the brilliant circle of the sun was beginning to rise in the east.

Slowly, infinitely slowly, the supporting skeleton arm of the maintenance tower began to fold back on its hinged base, leaving the rocket to stand alone.

It was a process which Salem Sharif knew would take time. Hopefully, enough time for the press corps jet to get clear.

Falcon reached the plane just as the last of the journalists were scrambling up the gangway. A handful of the terrorists were still following him and he turned to empty the last magazine in his AK-47 before he threw the weapon to one side. By then the gangway was empty and he hurried to push it to one side. Helen crouched in the open doorway above him and gave him covering fire to stop a final, dwindling rush of Kitaka's men.

Falcon jumped for the open doorway. Willing hands dragged him inside and the door was slammed shut behind him. He thanked his press colleagues with a brief grin, and then hurried forward to the flight deck. The pilot and co-pilot were already in their seats and the engines were running.

'All aboard,' Falcon informed them. 'Take her up and get us out of here quickly.'

The pilot nodded. He was too breathless to speak. He released the brakes, pushed forward the throttles, and the jet began to taxi forward for take-off.

At the far end of the runway the wreck of the MiG-17 was still blazing. Falcon swore as he realized that in the heat of the moment he had unwittingly put an obstacle in their path, but there was nothing he could do about it now. He could only hold tight and trust to the skill of the pilot.

The press corps jet hurtled to what seemed an unavoidable collision, and then at the last moment her nose lifted, the wheels cleared the runway, and they were airborne. The burning MiG-17 passed beneath them, close enough to scorch the rubber as their wheels retracted.

Sharif watched the jet plane take off as the rocket was cleared for launching. Then he turned back to watch the control panel and the TV image of *Vulcan One* as the countdown commenced from ten to zero.

At zero Jonas Kitaka pressed the red fire button. Huge beads of glistening sweat clung to his face, but the thick bush of his beard was again split by his beam of triumph.

Sharif folded his arms across his chest and his face was impassive as he waited out the last few seconds.

Allah would be his judge, and Allah was compassionate and all merciful. He clung to that thought.

Fire boiled and foamed at the base of the rocket, and slowly it started to ascend. In the final second it seemed to hover level with the tops of the nearest palm trees.

The warhead detonated and the blast from the radiating sunburst spun the press corps jet across the sky. Behind them the control centre and the remaining administration buildings were swallowed up. The entire launch site was razed flat and the atomic mushroom of red-veined cloud soared up into the pale blue sky. All around the diamond perimeter the jungle was a circle of fire.

The jet plane had been whirled like a toy in a gale, but when the air turbulence from the shock wave had passed it was still in one piece and the pilot was able to regain control. They had spiralled down to within fifty feet of the bush and treetops before he was able to pull her nose up and level her out. Then with a sigh of relief he began the climb back to safe altitude and the return flight to Salisbury.

The passengers had been badly shaken up and Helen had been thrown to the floor. Falcon helped her up and they stood together in the flight deck doorway. She was trembling and he put his arm around her and held her tight.

They had survived. They were alive.

But it was a long time before the trembling stopped.

A NOTE TO THE READER

Dear Reader,

Thank you for reading FIRESTRIKE. I hope you enjoyed reading it as much as I enjoyed writing it. Falcon's new role as a freelance photo journalist means that he is often in the right spot at the right time, and thus broadens the scope for storylines much wider than if I had kept him permanently in the SAS. His old boss is now working for MI5 and frequently calls upon him to use again all his old battle skills. In some missions he can be assigned military back up, and in others he will work alone. Either way you will be guaranteed a thrill a minute action adventure in one of the hottest parts of the globe.

I have written under other pen names and so my website is at **www.robertleaderauthor.com**. Go to **my Robert Charles page** for more information on my Robert Charles thrillers. My website was always meant to be reader friendly, with a full biography, a travel blog and notes on how each book came to be inspired and written. Please pay it a visit if you would like more information on Mark Falcon or anything else I have written.

In today's publishing world online reviews are vitally important and if you have enjoyed my work please spare the time to write a review for **Goodreads** and **Amazon**, or just a complimentary mention on any media platform.

If you want to contact me you can do so through **my website**. I am always pleased to hear from readers. In the meantime I will get on with the next Falcon SAS novel for your enjoyment.

Sincerely yours, Robert Charles

Sapere Books is an exciting new publisher of brilliant fiction and popular history.

To find out more about our latest releases and our monthly bargain books visit our website: **saperebooks.com**

Printed in Great Britain
by Amazon

20395180R00102